CULTS ON CAMPUS: CONTINUING CHALLENGE

Edited by

Marcia R. Rudin

American Family Foundation

An International Cult Education Program Book

Library of Congress Cataloging-in-Publication Data

Rudin, Marcia R., 1940 -
    Cults on campus: continuing challenge.

Library of Congress Catalog Card Number: 91-72497

ISBN 0-931337-02-X

About the Editor

Marcia R. Rudin is Director of the International Cult Education Program. She is co-author of *Why Me? Why Anyone?* and *Prison or Paradise? The New Religious Cults,* editor of *Young People and Cults: The Newsletter of the International Cult Education Program*, and writer and associate producer of the International Cult Education Program educational videotape, "Cults: Saying *No* Under Pressure."

About The Publisher

The **American Family Foundation** (AFF) is a nonprofit, tax-exempt research and educational organization founded in 1979 to assist cult victims and their families through the study of cultic groups and manipulative techniques of persuasion and control. AFF shares its findings with professionals, the general public, and those needing help with cultic involvements. AFF consists of a small professional staff and approximately 100 volunteer professionals including educators, psychiatrists, psychologists, social workers, sociologists, attorneys, clergy, business executives, journalists, physicians, law enforcement officials, college and university administrators, scientists, and others who contribute their efforts in the areas of research, education, the law, and victim assistance.

The **International Cult Education Program** (ICEP) helps professionals in colleges, universities, high schools, churches, synagogues, and other forums quickly and effectively educate themselves and their young people about cults, psychological manipulation, and satanism and occult ritual abuse. ICEP is building an active national and international network of professional and lay experts. ICEP provides programs, speakers, publications such as its semi-annual newsletter, *Young People and Cults*, and educational materials including a twenty-five minute videotape, "Cults: Saying *No* Under Pressure." The National Association of Student Personnel Administrators (NASPA) and the Association of College Unions-International (ACU-I) are ICEP Participating Organizations.

ICEP is a joint program of the American Family Foundation and the Cult Awareness Network. The **Cult Awareness Network** (CAN) is a national, non-profit corporation founded to educate the public about the harmful effects of mind control used by destructive cults. Although established as an organization by and for victims of cults, CAN members now include clergy, clinicians, educators, attorneys, law enforcement officials, and other professionals concerned about cults and mind control. CAN, a network of volunteers from approximately thirty affiliated groups in twenty states, confines its concerns to unethical or illegal practices and passes no judgment on doctrine or beliefs. CAN maintains a national office with a professional staff in Chicago, publishes a monthly newsletter, and sponsors national and regional conferences, seminars, and workshops.

Contributors

- **Gregory S. Blimling, Ph.D.**, Vice Chancellor for Student Development, Appalachian State University

- **Linda Osborne Blood**, co-author, *Satanism and Occult-Related Violence: What You Should Know;* former member, Temple of Set

- **Robert C. Fellows, MTS**, Educator/Mentalist/Magician; Author, *Easily Fooled: New Insights and Techniques for Resisting Manipulation*

- **Lorna Goldberg, MSW, ACSW**, New Jersey Institute for Training in Psychoanalysis

- **William Goldberg, MSW, ACSW**, Director, Community Support Center, Pomona, New York

- **Larry Kahaner**, KANE Associates International, Inc.; co-author, *How to Investigate Destructive Cults and Underground Groups* and author, *Cults That Kill*

- **Michael D. Langone, Ph.D.**, Executive Director, American Family Foundation; Editor, *Cultic Studies Journal;* co-author *Cults: What Parents Should Know* and *Satanism and Occult-Related Violence: What You Should Know*

- **Jane R. Lindley**, Sponsored Foreign Student Advisor, International Students and Scholars Office, Boston University

- **Ronald N. Loomis**, Director of Unions and Activities, Cornell University; Past President, Cult Awareness Network

- **Rev. Dr. Ross Miller**, Pastor, Trinity United Methodist Church, Eugene, Oregon

- **Dennis Polselli**, Staff Associate, Residence Life, Framingham State College

- **Carl J. Rheins, Ph.D.**, Dean, Student Life and Development, Adelphi University

- **Herbert L. Rosedale, Esq.**, Senior Partner, Parker, Chapin, Flatteau & Klimpl; President, American Family Foundation

- **Marcia R. Rudin, MA**, Director, International Cult Education Program; Editor, *Young People and Cults;* co-author, *Prison or Paradise? The New Religious Cults*

- **Patricia E. Ryan**, President, Cult Awareness Network

- **Rev. Robert Watts Thornburg**, Dean, Marsh Chapel, Boston University

- **Larry Zilliox, Jr.**, KANE Associates International, Inc.; co-author, *How to Investigate Destructive Cults and Underground Groups*

Acknowledgements

I want to thank everyone who offered their advice and assistance in the preparation of this book.

I want to especially thank

.   Daniel A. Silver for his design and execution of the book's cover;

.   Ian Quinn for his technical and proofreading assistance;

.   Michael D. Langone, Michael J. Caslin, and Herbert L. Rosedale, Esq. for their guidance and support; and

.   my husband, Rabbi James Rudin, and my daughters, Eve and Jennifer, for their patience.

Marcia R. Rudin,
Editor
Spring, 1991

Contents

Robert C. Fellows, MTS
(reprinted with permission from *Easily Fooled:*
New Insights and Techniques for Resisting
Manipulation, Mind Matters, (c) 1989,
and with permission from American
Family Foundation)

How to Talk to People Who are Trying to Save You
Rev. Dr. Ross Miller
(adapted from an article originally appearing
in, and reprinted with permission from, *Yellow*
Sheet, September 1983, and reprinted with
permission from American Family Foundation)

VI. **Resources**
Marcia R. Rudin, MA

Why This Book?

When parents send their children off to a college or university their anxieties know no bounds. Will their youngsters be able to handle their new-found independence? Will they be lonely? Will they fall prey to substance abuse? Can they handle sexual freedom responsibly? Will they be able to withstand increased pressures and expectations?

Today, parents and university executives, counselors, campus clergy, and others concerned about the welfare and quality of life for students on campuses are overwhelmed with serious issues they must confront at their institutions such as racism, anti-Semitism, sexism, date- and acquaintance-rape, campus crime, youth suicides, and the frightening new specter of AIDS. The last thing parents and college and university staff and administrators need is another problem or issue affecting the welfare of their youngsters.

Unfortunately, cults on campus are one more thing for us to worry about, one more--and a major--threat to the welfare, human rights, and indeed the very futures of our students. Cults can disrupt and often destroy lives, can sometimes impair or permanently damage intellectual abilities. Cults threaten the very reason our youngsters attend institutions of higher learning because these groups are generally anti-intellectual and often force students to drop out of school. They oppose freedom of thought and discourse, which is the very basis for our educational system.

"Cults. . . haven't they gone away?" That's what cult experts tell me they usually hear when the subject comes up. No, they haven't gone away. They are now more numerous than ever, more sophisticated in their recruiting methods than before, and, as life becomes more complex and difficult for our young people, even stronger in their appeal.

Higher education executives need to learn about cults and how to protect their schools. *Cults on Campus: Continuing Challenge* is an important book that addresses an urgent topic in a practical way.

Carl J. Rheins, Ph.D.
Dean, Student Life and Development
Adelphi University

Introduction

Herbert L. Rosedale, Esq. and Patricia E. Ryan

In 1987, the American Family Foundation (AFF) and the National Association of Student Personnel Administrators (NASPA) jointly published a slim volume, *Cultism on Campus: Commentaries and Guidelines for College and University Administrators.* That book helped create widespread awareness among college administrators and staff, as well as the general public, of the problems caused by destructive groups and helped thousands of institutions respond knowledgeably and constructively to the challenge of cults on their campuses.

Although that book was published only four years ago, the rapidly-changing cult scene on campuses and the urgent need for current information has prompted publication of this new group of essays.

The Phenomenon

Cults are still a serious problem on campuses. Cult recruiters continue to operate on campus grounds and in dormitories, student lounges, dining halls, libraries, and other gathering places. Cult groups attempt to establish themselves as campus clubs or other official student activities; some attempt to gain entry into campus ministry organizations. Some cults may not be accurate about the official level of support they enjoy from the institution and may represent themselves as having more official status than they do. Professors--often those hired as adjuncts--or other staff members may recruit through their classes, counseling sessions, or other activities, inviting students to Bible study sessions, for example. Indeed, says William Goldberg in the book's first essay, "Cults on Campus: How Can you Help?," today's campuses are often a kind of "spiritual supermarket" where "students are promised universal cures, unqualified happiness, guaranteed salvation and magically-attained wealth by thousands of destructive cults."

However, the cult scene on campuses, as everywhere else, is changing rapidly. It is now often harder to spot cult-recruitment activity because the groups do not appear to be as counterculture-oriented as in the past. Business or management-training cults, political cults, psychotherapy groups, and mass mind-empowerment therapeutic cults are now recruiting on campuses as well as religious cults. And many cults that are religious organizations now have the appearance of mainstream religious groups. Most religious cults on campuses today have conventional, orthodox theologies, and this makes it harder for students as well as administrators and staff to recognize a group as harmful. (It is the use of deception and unethical manipulation, not a group's theology or ideas, that qualifies a group as a destructive cult; this is the definition of cults employed by the American Family Foundation.)

Recently, cults have stepped up their efforts to attract students from other countries studying on American campuses. Jane Lindley, in her essay, "Cult Recruitment of International Students on American Campuses," explains why foreign students are vulnerable to cult recruitment and what the international student educator can do to prevent it.

In the last few years campus administrators have become concerned about students practicing satanism and other occult rituals. Many campus security administrators and other campus staff members are training themselves to spot signs of occult activity and crime. In "Satanism and Young People: What Educators Should Know," Linda Blood and Dr. Michael Langone assess the prevalence of youth satanism, explain why young people are attracted to it, list satanic activities and their effects, and outline possible signs of involvement.

Policy and Legal Issues

What can colleges and universities do about cults on campus? Even if the college administrators spot cult activity on their campuses, it is difficult for them to deal with cult recruiters, particularly if their institution is a public one. In his comprehensive essay, "The Involvement of College Students in Totalist Groups: Causes, Concerns, Legal Issues, and Policy Considerations," Dr. Gregory Blimling carefully analyzes the legal issues involved in working with cults on campus. He discusses the right of student religious organizations to use university facilities for religious purposes, religious proselytizing, religious conduct, and recognition of religious student organizations by the college or university.

Another method of monitoring cult recruitment on campuses is to convince all religious groups operating there to adhere to a previously agreed-upon ethical code when approaching students. In "Developing an Ethical Code for Proselytizers," Marcia Rudin describes the program undertaken by Rev. Robert Watts Thornburg of Boston University, the American Family Foundation, and various representatives of Evangelical and other religious groups to design a document that will "provide a useful guide to those concerned about cult recruitment at their schools and will help ensure that campus religious activity falls within publicly agreed-upon ethical guidelines."

Training Campus Staff and Educating Students

The most effective way to meet the continuing challenge of cults on campus is through intensive preventive education and staff training. In "Training Residence-Hall Staff," Rev. Robert Thornburg offers practical advice and detailed guidelines for utilizing campus residence staff to provide effective cult-education programs to students and for training them to recognize signs of cult involvement. Dennis Polselli complements Rev. Thornburg's contribution in "Why Resident Assistant Training on Cultism?"

Campus chaplains, counselors, and other staff members may find themselves in the difficult position of having to advise and counsel parents of cult victims and help them cope with their family member's cultic involvement. Psychologist Michael Langone shares his professional counseling insights in his essay, "Working with Cult-Affected Families." In "Counseling the Cult-Impacted Student," therapists Lorna Goldberg and William Goldberg advise college staff who may face the task of counseling students who are being recruited into a cult, may be actively involved in a cult, or are thinking of leaving a group.

Since campus law-enforcement administrators are often those most closely in touch with what's happening on campus grounds, they need to learn how to identify cult recruiters and how to spot unusual and possibly harmful or destructive activities. In "How Campus Law Enforcement Personnel Can Monitor Cult Activities," Larry Kahaner and Larry Zilliox, Jr. offer practical advice such as closely examining the material groups pass out on campus.

Finally, continuous education of students must be undertaken by colleges and universities if cult recruitment is to be curbed. In "A Multi-Faceted Approach to Preventive-Education Programs about Cults" Ronald Loomis recounts how he organizes year-long cult-education programs at Cornell University. Marcia Rudin describes another university's extensive cult-education program in "University of California - Berkeley's Cult Awareness Efforts."

The texts of two short pamphlets designed for students as hand-outs complete the student-education section. "When You're Asked About Cults" is written by Robert Fellows, who presents educational, experiential workshops about mind manipulation for students. In "How to Talk to People Who Are Trying to Save You," Rev. Dr. Ross Miller tells students how to resist aggressive proselytizers with tact and sensitivity.

Resources

This compendium of resources lists periodicals, brochures, books, reports, information packets, curricula and other teaching aids, and audio-visual resources currently available. An extensive list of resource organizations throughout the world enables the reader to obtain additional information and assistance.

Cults on Campus: The Phenomenon

Cults on Campus: How Can You Help?

William Goldberg, MSW, ACSW

The college campuses of the 1990's are different from the campuses of the 1960's, when radical politics, mass demonstrations, teach-ins, and marches presented special problems for campus administrators and staff. Today, for the most part, campuses appear to be quieter. This calm is deceptive, however, because today's campuses face some challenges that were neither as potent nor as widespread thirty years ago. One of these challenges involves the destructive organizations capitalizing on the frustrations, fears, anxieties, and needs of today's college students, leading them to work against their own interests as well as the interests of society.

Today's campus has been characterized as a "spiritual supermarket." Students are promised universal cures, unqualified happiness, guaranteed salvation, and magically-attained wealth by thousands of destructive cults. These cults pressure the students to abandon their families, friends, and futures in order to follow an individual who claims to have discovered the path to perfection.

College campuses are the chief recruiting centers of most destructive cults, and virtually every college campus in the country has been and continues to be visited by these organizations. This article will identify the cultists, describe their actions, discuss the reasons why they find college campuses particularly rich for recruiting purposes, and suggest ways that campus administrators and staff can properly intervene to protect the students and the college.

The most damaging myth is that people who join destructive cults are seekers by nature and that if they did not fall into a destructive cult, they would probably look for some other way to escape the pressures of the real world. In fact, most cultists are normal, healthy individuals with the typical kinds of problems that young people today encounter.

As Dr. Margaret Thaler Singer, Adjunct Professor of Psychology at the University of California - Berkeley, puts it, "The myth is that the potential cultists are like tourists searching everywhere for the Washington Monument. If they don't find it here, they'll look elsewhere until they find what they're seeking."

Actually, Dr. Singer points out, there are hundreds of these "Washington

Monuments" on the campus today, constantly looking for vulnerable young people. For the most part, cultists do not hear a philosophy and then decide to join the group which has that philosophy. Instead, they see a group that seems to have something they want (such as love, purpose, determination and direction) and, in order to become part of that group, they adopt its philosophy.

The reason I emphasize this fact is that if campus staff whose responsibility it is to watch out for the welfare of the students see potential cultists as individuals who are searching for a way to escape responsibility no matter what, they might not recognize the importance of their timely intervention. The intervention may be just what the student needs to keep from getting involved in the first place.

The first questions to ask, of course, are, "What are destructive cults?" and "Just what is being destroyed?" A destructive cult is a group that deceives potential recruits into believing that it is something it is not; it then pressures, manipulates and isolates the recruit from the familiar guideposts; and, finally, it introduces a doctrine that the group claims will fit every circumstance and clarify all doubts and confusion. The reason the doctrine may seem to answer a recruit's concerns is that the individual has been worn down through a system of marathon sessions, manipulation of vulnerabilities (e.g., the need to be liked and the desire to be seen as open-minded), and love-bombing to the point where simplistic black-and-white superficialities appear to be profound utterances of truth. What is being destroyed is the individual's critical senses.

Due to a desire to be seen as good group members, cultists learn to muffle the part of themselves that is uneasy with the cult's philosophy and actions and, instead, to believe and act without question. Indeed, one of the major features of the destructive cult is that this type of group will advise their adherents to give up their egos, to *surrender* to the general sense of right and wrong, to accept that which they would have rejected had they not been placed into a state of heightened suggestibility and narrowed consciousness. As they come to embrace the notion that doubt is satanically inspired and that the only acceptable stance is one of childlike acceptance, the cultists learn to distrust their instincts.

There are many different types of groups that use the techniques mentioned above, but most of them fit into one of four categories.

1.   Religious cults: These are the best known of the groups. The leader is

seen by those in the cult as a god or one who has a direct and unique relationship with God. Only he/she can interpret the word of God Group members are usually taught to define the world in terms of an imminent Armageddon. Only the members of their particular group will be saved, while all non-believers will perish.

2. Therapy cults: These groups are similar to religious cults, except that they worship a leader not because of his/her relationship with God, but because the leader has reached some ill-defined point of psychological perfection. The goal of the therapy cultist is not to be saved and, therefore, free of sin, but to be cured and, therefore, free of hang-ups. The words are different, but the recruitment, the message, and the elusive goals are the same.

3. Political cults: In these groups, the leader is an individual who has the perfect political doctrine. Again, he/she is flawless and has discovered some great truth. Again, the world is coming to see that the leader's way is the only path to follow and the Upheaval will occur sometime soon. Those who are enlightened early will be in the vanguard of the movement as it sweeps the world. Extremist groups and domestic terrorist organizations have often been described as cult-like in their methods and in the effect they have on their members.

4. Economic cults: The appeal in these groups is material success. By abandoning one's plans and goals and following the leader, the cultist is promised future fortune. As with the other categories, the recruit is put through a series of pressures and manipulations, and is isolated from friends and family. As with the other groups, the end point of this process is a demand for an immediate and total commitment or the loss of the opportunity for financial success forever.

As one can see, the goals, rewards, or philosophy of these groups may be somewhat different, but the overall themes are the same: If you give up your plans, ideas, and individuality and blindly follow our leader, he/she will make you holy, healthy, enlightened, or rich. There is only one path, and our leader has found it. Anyone who disagrees with our doctrine is doomed to a life of sin, ignorance, neurosis, or failure.

The end result of cultic manipulation has been called brainwashing, mind control, thought reform, information disease, and coercive persuasion. These terms describe an experience that leads the individual to make sudden major changes in lifestyle, opinions, ethics, sense of loyalty, and view of the world. The cult member assumes a new identity and is often given a new name and a new "re-birth day" to further emphasize the break with the past.

The process that leads to these changes is usually accomplished after the new recruit is away from the campus, in a new environment. The "hook" which leads the individual to enter that environment is often conventional and mild--the desire to meet new people, to be exposed to new ideas, or to hear a new point of view. Once the potential recruit is in the new environment, though, he/she is lectured, cajoled, infantilized and undermined. Resistance to suggestions is gradually worn down and, as it erodes, knowledge of the group's purpose, real philosophy, and real leadership is permitted to increase. Outsiders are given derogatory labels (e.g. Systemites, Karmis, Products of the Fallen World). The potential recruit is told that this is the only chance to join in the New Age. The most important movement in history is occurring right now in this group, and the potential recruit can be part of it! All he/she has to do is surrender, turn off the mind, banish satanic thoughts, etc. The world is seen in blacks and whites. There is no gray, and there is no other acceptable path.

In their book, *Snapping*, Flo Conway and Jim Siegelman state that there is usually a single moment of conversion, which is an intense experience that has been engineered, but which is interpreted as proof of the truth of the cult's teaching. This experience is seen as the entry of the Holy Spirit, or becoming enlightened, or finding "it." It is, however, a predictable response to the series of manipulations that the individual has experienced.

Of course, there are several reasons why the cults do most of their recruiting on college campuses. Although college students are not the only ones vulnerable to the appeal of the cults, they are in a circumstance that is particularly conducive to the cults' appeals. Many of the students are away from home for the first time--or at least on their own and totally responsible for themselves for the first time--in their lives. Parents are no longer watching over the student, and their colleges do not take as much of a personal interest in the students as their high schools did. There is a sense of release and power which comes with that freedom, but as with all such freedom, there is also a sense of fear and discomfort. The removal of parental boundaries is both desired and secretly feared by most college students. They are simultaneously rebelling against parental authority and uncertain of what will happen to them when it is removed. Along comes the cult leader, who gives the potential recruit a way to simultaneously rebel against authority and not have to accept responsibility for his/her own life. The new recruit can merely transfer dependency, thus rebelling against the parents while still not having to accept total adult responsibility.

The pressures on college students come from many sources. They can be academic, social, sexual, and/or financial. This is a time in life when people feel particularly insecure and alone. Parents are not there to provide structure, limits, and a sounding board for many different new ideas. This is a time of crossroad decisions in the students' lives. They are deciding upon careers, lifestyles, sexual preferences, and identity. Adolescence is the primary transition stage of adulthood and, therefore, the primary stage of vulnerability to someone speaking with authority who says, "If you follow me, you won't have to make those crossroad decisions. I'll make them for you and free you from the burden." As outsiders watching the drama, we recognize that the price the recruit will have to pay for that "freedom" is tremendous but, to a temporarily insecure individual, immediate relief from pressure can be seen as a desirable result.

Many cults solidify this process by controlling access to information that may be critical of the cult and its techniques. Often, cultists are told to cut off ties with their families and other people whom they knew prior to entering the cult so that they will not be "contaminated" by the unenlightened views of these individuals.

Of course, late adolescence is also a time of relatively few attachments and roots. The students used to be able to answer the question, "Who are you?" with the statement, "I am my parent's child." They no longer wish to adopt their primary identity from their relationship to their parents, but they have not yet fully developed an answer to this question. They may seek to answer, if temporarily, by becoming a member of a movement: "Who am I? I am an anti-nuke demonstrator (or vegetarian, or environmentalist, etc.)."

Another factor that enters into the vulnerability of the college student is that college education is traditionally an experience of trying on new ideologies and ideas. Beliefs held since childhood are challenged and modified. This is a necessary part of learning to think with a critical mind, but there is a period of uncertainty and vulnerability when these old ideas are challenged. The potential recruit is most vulnerable to cults during this period.

At this point, I would like to focus on the ways that campus staff can offer help. As stated in the introduction to this article, potential cultists are generally not single-mindedly looking for a cult experience. Instead, they are usually tricked into coming away for a period of time and are then manipulated into joining the group. The campus staff can be helpful right from the initial stage--the encounter with a cult recruiter on campus. Often, an otherwise intelligent individual can be seduced into abandoning his/her critical faculties during such an encounter.

I had the experience of waiting for a plane in Newark International Airport last year. As I was waiting, I noticed a pretty young woman walking up to men, smiling broadly at them, pinning an American flag pin onto their lapel, and asking for a donation. After I saw a few men give her money, I started to walk around the airport with her. When she went into her act, and as each of the men reached for his wallet, I called out, "Do you know what organization she represents?" Each time I asked this elementary question, the men would ask her, find out that she was a member of a cult, put their wallets back, and walk away.

The point of this anecdote is not that these men were any more gullible than you or me. The point is that, in that moment, when they were face-to-face with a pretty young girl who had given them something, they did not have the strength to seem like a skinflint and say "no" to her request for money or to seem mistrustful and to ask her for some identification. When I "gave permission" to ask appropriate questions, they were able to do so. All it took was a logical question from someone who was not captured by this young women's seeming innocence. Anyone who has had the experience of buying something from a fast-talking salesperson, only to realize later that the item really wasn't needed, will understand how people can be led into an atmosphere of suggestibility.

When I speak to college students, I often recommend that before they agree to leave for a retreat with any organization they haven't heard of, they should check with the campus police. If the group is what it purports to be, it will have a reputation. Campus law-enforcement administrators, on the receiving end of these requests for information, can be a great deal of help to potential cult victims by finding out about new groups on campus and telling inquiring students what they know.

I am not suggesting, of course, that every new group on campus is a cult. But asking where the group has other chapters and placing a telephone call to a colleague at another college may turn up some information that could save a student from a tragic mistake.

When a student asks you for advice regarding a group, you can recommend questions that should be answered before they agree to go away with a recruiter. Ironically, individuals who would never buy a new car or a stereo system without reading about it, speaking to others who own one, and asking critical questions, can agree to give up their time, money and, potentially, their lives without asking enough questions. Whereas people may be wary of a salesperson who is trying to talk them into buying a material object, there is an assumption that a salesperson who is trying to talk them into buying a philosophy does not use the same techniques and devices. Thousands of former cultists can attest to the fact that this assumption is wrong.

You can suggest that the following questions be asked, or, if you come across a cult recruiter on your campus, you can ask these questions yourself:

1. Is your organization known by any other name?

2. Who is the leader of your organization?

3. Can you give me the names of other students who have been to one of your retreats?

4. Does your organization operate on other college campuses? Which ones?

5. If someone decides he/she wants to leave before the seminar is over, how can he/she get back here?

6. Why have you chosen to recruit members by speaking to them on street corners rather than more traditional ways of recruiting?

7. Exactly where is the retreat and how else (other than your bus) can people get there and leave?

8. How does your group get its money?

Of course, cultists define their standards of right and wrong in terms of what benefits their mission. Therefore, whether the recruiter will answer truthfully is problematic. There is no instant litmus test to distinguish cults from other groups. I am recommending that you suggest these questions to the students less as a means of finding whether they will be given the "right" answers than so that you can model a critical attitude for them in order to help them see that asking questions and being skeptical is an acceptable (and perhaps wise) stance to take.

I would advise students to be particularly wary of groups that claim that they cannot explain their philosophy unless the student comes away with them or that the philosophy cannot be put into words. ("How do you explain ice cream to someone who has never tasted it?") If the message is that the potential recruit has to leave the familiar environment and *experience* the situation rather than have it explained, emotional manipulation may be an important element of that experience.

In the long run, the best defense against dishonest, manipulative recruiting by cults is the truth. And the truth can best be served when all the facts about the group, its purposes, and its leadership are brought into the open.

Cult Recruitment of International Students on American Campuses

Jane R. Lindley

These are my memories of the words I heard four years ago from Maria, a seventeen year-old freshman at Boston University from the Philippines. It was the first time as a foreign student advisor that I heard a student describe an encounter with what we now understand to be a destructive religious group.

I didn't know how to say "no" to them. They were so friendly. They were the first Americans to invite me to dinner.

I had been sitting by myself in the cafeteria when a young girl came over to sit with me. She asked me where I was from and what I was studying. She seemed interested in me. Then she invited me to go to dinner that evening with her friends. I was so happy--I had been feeling very lonely, I was missing my family in the Philippines.

We had a wonderful dinner. Then, after dinner, everyone got together to read the Bible. I felt that was strange, but it was still interesting. I got together with these people a few more times, but the situation felt more and more strange. I did not really have the time to visit with them as much as they wanted me to because my classes were demanding more homework and I was going to have mid-term examinations soon. I tried to explain this to them. I thought they were also students and they would understand, but they did not seem to, and they just kept calling and insisting.

I didn't know how to say "no." They had been so friendly, and in my country declining invitations from friends is considered to be rude. I was also feeling increasingly uncomfortable with the discussions about religion. To me, religion is a very private part of my life. I am a Catholic, and though I was interested in knowing about other religions, particularly about religious practices in the United States, I felt a certain pressure from the group to believe what they believed. Finally I told them I had too much studying to do and I could not go to all of these dinners with them. Even though they continued to phone me, I didn't go. I felt so impolite! I never saw any of them again.

Maria was fortunate because she did not get seriously involved with the organization trying to recruit her. However, her experience was clearly a disturbing one for her, as it was her first social encounter with a group of Americans. She had been put in an uncomfortable situation in which she felt she was going against her cultural norms of being polite and showing respect to her hosts. The incident also had the unfortunate outcome of making her suspicious of genuinely friendly overtures from others.

The international student can be considered easy prey for cult groups for any one of the following reasons:

1. They are often alone and homesick, particularly when they first arrive in the United States.

2. They are usually governed by cultural norms which dictate politeness.

3. They are out of their own cultural milieu and have a difficult time discerning genuine overtures of friendship.

4. They are eager to learn about the host country's customs, and therefore welcome the opportunity to meet Americans.

International Hospitality Programs

Finding families or individuals to serve as hosts to foreign students is one of the international student educator's most challenging tasks. These hosts offer personal contacts, hospitality, and friendship to international students, sharing American culture and providing educational enrichment opportunities outside of the classroom. Host families do such things as taking the students out for dinner and entertaining them at holiday times.

Approximately 80% of the hosts currently in our program are church-affiliated. Each one of the churches represented has a coordinator who serves as a liaison between the church and the International Students and Scholars Office. These coordinators are familiar with the National Association for Foreign Student Affairs (NAFSA) Guidelines for hosting international students*, and either in a group forum or on an individual basis, inform the hosts about the need to adhere strictly to these guidelines.

But it is the other 20% of the individuals or families not familiar with the guidelines who apply to be hosts which cause the most concern to me. For the most part, these potential hosts are genuinely interested in extending hospitality to the international student. Their interests may simply be altruistic, they may wish to expose their children to a new culture, or they may want to exchange language classes.

Our concern at the International Students and Scholars Office is how to spot the host who is a cult member, or, even better, how to prevent this individual or family from becoming one of our hosts. This is truly a matter of detective work because the cult member does not identify him/herself as such. That is where the insidiousness begins. The cult member is usually very enthusiastic and is willing to go the extra mile to welcome the students, whether by picking them up from the airport or hosting them at his/her home until the students find housing. For those of us working with international students, these offers of support can be very inviting, particularly today when recruiting volunteers for any job is so difficult.

What Can International Student Educators Do?

We need to use a sixth sense and be aware of clues to discover the true intentions of those offering assistance. While this may smack of elitism or over-suspiciousness, it is our responsibility to protect the students to the best of our ability. Clues to look for include use of correspondence stationery bearing the name of a group or a sudden increase in host family applications, especially in those applicants using one name as a reference.

If you don't know the person who makes the referral of the host family, call him/her. Try to find out in what way the host-family applicants are connected to the person making the referral.

Since there is no scientific way to assign students to host families, you must often follow your intuition. If you strongly suspect that the host applicant is a cult member, eliminate him/her from your pool of volunteers or approach him/her directly and try to discern any suspicious affiliations.

For the student's protection, make sure he/she is assigned to one of the Hospitality Program Coordinators. You should make clear to the student that if he/she feels the least bit uncomfortable with the host assigned, whether it is because the host is insistent about attending religious services or for other reasons, the coordinator will be responsible for removing the student from that situation.

Both as a participant in a Host Family Program or as a member of the university community, the student should feel that he/she has resources for genuine support. Students should be apprised of these available resources as soon as they enroll at the university. Information packets should contain written materials on the recruitment tactics of destructive religious organizations. Names and phone numbers of university staff such as International Student Office personnel, campus ministers, mental-health professionals, trained student leaders, and resident advisors should be made available to the international student in case he/she is approached by a cult recruiter, gets involved with a cult, or generally has any questions.

Most importantly, however, you should offer educational workshops about cults during mandatory international student-orientation sessions. These have proven to be most effective means of protecting foreign students. Well-informed speakers need to impart clear information about the presence, practices, and recruitment methods of destructive groups on campus.

* In 1989 the Board of Directors of the National Association for Foreign Student Affairs (NAFSA), the organization of professionals working with international students in American colleges and universities and with American students studying abroad, adopted a Code of Ethics for its members. One section of this Code of Ethics addresses the problem of proselytizing of foreign students: "Members with responsibilities in community organizations working with foreign students and scholars shall. . .provide adequate orientation for volunteers and participants in community programs so they may interact constructively. The orientation should make clear that proselytizing (that is, manipulating, applying pressure, or offering special inducements to effect a change in religious or philosophical beliefs) is unacceptable."

Satanism and Young People:
What Educators Should Know

Linda Osborne Blood and Michael D. Langone, Ph.D.

How Prevalent is Satanism?

No reliable scientific data can tell us how many persons are involved in satanism, black magic, and related practices, but a most disturbing trend has been the apparent increased interest in satanism among the young.

Epidemiological data indicate that 20% of the population have some kind of psychiatric disorder (Freedman, 1986). Evidence of satanic rituals involving youth has been found in all areas of the country. One study found that 8 of 250 adolescents (3.2%) referred for psychiatric help to a facility that handled all adolescent psychiatric referrals for a particular geographic area were involved in satanism and related forms of occultism (Bourget *et al.*, 1988), and another study reported that 17 of 32 adolescent referrals were involved (Wheeler *et al.*, 1988). If referrals to an adolescent psychiatric facility came from the most disturbed 20% of those 20% who are diagnosable, then perhaps .12% of adolescents could be seriously involved in satanism and psychiatrically disturbed. We can only assume that many who are not part of the psychiatric population are also involved.

Although this is a very small percentage, it would translate, if true, into thousands, perhaps tens of thousands, of cases. One should remember, however, that in many, and probably in most, of these cases, the satanic involvement may be shallow, or peripheral to other, more serious, difficulties.

Another, though less persuasive, approach toward estimating prevalence can be based upon extrapolations from the numbers of youth attracted to heavy-metal rock music, some of which has been viewed as encouraging interest in satanism. According to Gallup polls (Gallup Youth Survey Release, March 22, 1989), 27% of teens enjoy listening to hard rock/heavy-metal music more than other kinds of music. Another study, reported by Pulling (1989; Wass, H., findings published in *The Influence of Media on Adolescents*), showed that 90% of the students surveyed reported being rock fans, of whom approximately 9% of the urban middle school students, 17% of the rural, and 24% of the urban high school students were identified as "HSS [homicide, suicide, satanic practices] fans." About 20% of the students surveyed overall reported that they always agree with the words to their favorite rock music.

Other Gallup polls (Gallup Youth Survey Release, October 26, 1988) find substantial teen belief in angels (74%) and witchcraft (29%). (Unfortunately, Gallup has not yet asked questions specifically related to belief in Satan.) And still other polls (Gallup Youth Survey Release, May 10, 1989) reveal that approximately one-third of teens who are regular attendees at Protestant or Catholic churches believe in reincarnation, a belief rejected by Christianity but upheld by most Eastern and New Age religious philosophies. The findings of these various polls indicate that a large minority of teens a) are not very well grounded in their religions, b) believe in witchcraft and--by extension from their opinions on angels and witchcraft--the Devil, and c) are attracted to heavy-metal music. If even one or two percent of these teens were seriously influenced by satanism, the total number would be in the tens of thousands.

It is vital, however, that one not overreact to these speculative estimates. Even if tens of thousands of teens were adversely affected by satanism, it does not follow that tens of thousands of teens are involved in child sacrifice, murder, drug dealing, and similarly lurid aspects of satanism. The overwhelming majority of teens involved in satanism appear to be participating at what has been called the "dabbler" level, that is, they have developed a fascination with satanism but have maintained enough of their rational faculties and social inhibitions to avoid its violent and perverted aspects. Perhaps for many of these teens, dabbling in satanism is a transient form of power fantasy that sustains a fragile ego on the rocky road of growing up, similar to another era's teen fantasies of joining a motorcycle gang.

Nonetheless, even if a tiny percentage of teens becomes deeply involved in satanism, the consequences to them and to those whose lives they touch can be terrible. This is not a problem that should be dismissed out-of-hand.

Why do People Get Involved in Satanism?

Most experts in the field divide practitioners of satanism into four categories: 1) "dabblers," usually teenagers who become attracted to satanism on a relatively superficial level through easily-available books, heavy-metal music, fantasy role-playing games, and the like; 2) "self-styled" or "psychopathic" satanists, usually loners attracted to the more violent forms of satanism which are then grafted onto their pre-existing pathology; 3) "religious" satanists involved in well-organized, publicly-acknowledged groups such as the Church of Satan or Temple of Set, and 4) "satanic cults," the sophisticated, clandestine groups which may be engaged in criminal activities. There is some overlap among these categories, but the system of classification appears to be of use in determining type and level of involvement (Tucker, 1989).

Although hard data are lacking, police and mental health reports (Markowitz, 1989; Murphy and Zilliox, 1989; Tucker, 1989) suggest that most adolescents involved in satanism are dabblers--usually boys between 9 and 19 years of age who are experimenting with satanic activities but are not fully committed to satanism. Their rituals may include animal mutilation and sacrifice, drinking blood, eating animal organs, drug abuse, and self-mutilation. They may engage in vandalism, theft, arson, and other illegal activities.

Dabblers are often alienated, troubled teens with low self-esteem who exhibit problems with aggressive behavior and/or suicidal tendencies, both of which can be aggravated by involvement in satanism. They may come from working-, upper-, or middle-class backgrounds, and are often from dysfunctional families. Many are bright, creative, and intellectually curious but are usually underachievers and loners who do poorly in school and/or have learning disabilities. Some satanist dabblers are street kids whose involvement is usually tied in with drugs, especially PCP and LSD (personal communication, Sandi Gallant, January 4, 1989), and heavy-metal music, rather than intellectual curiosity about the occult. They may be bored and rebellious, but they also feel the need to belong and may be vulnerable to influence by strong, charismatic personalities. Many display an angry, hedonistic, and nihilistic attitude. Also, the incidence of serious psychological disorders seems to be significantly higher in teens who become involved in satanism than in those who join other types of cults.

Teenagers often become involved with satanic cults because the rituals appear to confer magical power, especially since many practitioners of satanism tend to claim that everything that happens to their benefit is the result of magic and/or the power of Satan (Scott, 1984). Scientific illiteracy and the popularity of the New Age Movement have contributed to a resurgence of belief in and fascination with pseudoscience, paranormal claims, occultism, and "transpersonal" experiences among young people, as the Gallup polls cited earlier indicate. While most of this fascination is expressed in relatively harmless ways, Tucker (1989) observed that young people who participated in intense satanic rituals--especially where drugs are involved--sometimes become entranced and experience out-of-body states or see visions and hear voices which they interpret as manifestations of Satan or demons. These experiences may subsequently exert a profound influence on the young person's paradigm of reality. In addition, some youths speak of achieving a "high" during certain satanic ceremonies (especially those involving the torture and sacrifice of animals) which they experience as a "powerful urge to harm." Tucker likens this euphoria to the "power rush" celebrated in the darker forms of heavy-metal music--those which emphasize ritual killing and mutilation--and expresses concern that some teens may actually learn to enjoy sadistic acts via those experiences.

Teens who are alienated from or rebelling against mainstream religion may find that satanism provides an outlet for their religious needs. Many teens are first introduced to the satanist belief system through Church of Satan founder Anton LaVey's *Satanic Bible*. Tucker (1989) notes that LaVey's book "advocates a kind of fierce independence that includes anarchy, rebellion, and radical self-sufficiency to teens at a time in their lives when attitudes toward authority are being shaped" (p. 3), and that the book's militantly anti-authority tone can be very attractive to adolescents.

LaVey also champions the free expression of aggressive and sexual drives--although he is careful to avoid advocacy of criminal acts--and glorifies the acquisition of power over others. He "offers a picture of reality in which humanity is portrayed as an advanced form of vicious animal, in which the weak are overwhelmed by the strong, and in which sentiments such as love, compassion, and warmth are the attributes of the weak. The vision is a mixture of Darwinism and a form of Machiavellianism combined with elements of the Nietzschean 'will to power'" (Tucker, 1989, p. 4). LaVey's worldview comes across as "honest" and "realistic" to some teenagers who see adult society as characterized by violence, hypocrisy, greed, and corruption. In addition, some may feel that they can get more out of life if they can learn to control others through fear.

Clinicians suggest that satanism and black magic can also feed into pre-existing problems and conflicts. Teens who feel powerless, victimized, and isolated may find that satanism provides a sense of control, status, and belonging. Intense group identity and bonding may result when a cult forms around a charismatic peer or adult who acts as high priest. Some participants may be attracted by the chance to act out their anger and frustration, indulge in antisocial behavior, or satisfy their sexual urges. Others, trapped in abusive home situations, may turn to magic in the hope that it will offer them a way to defend themselves and gain control of their lives. Adolescents who are trying to cope with their conflicts through delinquency and drug or alcohol abuse may find that satanism provides a rationale for their behavior as well as yet another form of escapism. Even relatively well-adjusted teens may have an inner fantasy life of which parents are unaware but which may make them vulnerable to some of the images of satanism such as power, violence, sexuality, mystery, and "sword-and-sorcery" mythology and romanticism.

While most teens who become involved in satanism are boys, girls who dabble in "white witchcraft" but want to move on to something more powerful may be lured into black magic. Others may be victimized by siblings or boyfriends who have become involved with cults, or by predatory adults (Pulling, 1989).

How Does Satanic Involvement Affect People?

Teens who become involved in satanism often display diminished intellectual ability. Grades may plummet as the teenager becomes obsessed with the occult and loses interest in achieving goals through any means other than magic.

Obsession with satanism or involvement with a violence-oriented satanist cult may lead an individual to rationalize participation in antisocial, violent, and/or criminal acts such as vandalism, animal sacrifice, arson, rape, drug or alcohol abuse, theft, blackmail, extortion, suicide, and murder. Teenagers dabbling in satanism may become involved with adult satanist cults and be manipulated or blackmailed into serious criminal activity.

Satanism in increasingly seen as a factor in suicide among teenagers. Some have left notes stating that they killed themselves in order to meet Satan, who would grant them reincarnation as powerful beings with control over demons; some had even made pacts with Satan to kill themselves by a certain date. In a few cases, teenagers involved in satanist cults have threatened their parents with mass suicide if they interfered.

Involvement in satanism may destroy relationships with family and friends. Parents and friends report a high incidence of alienation among satanic cult members, sometimes manifesting itself in outright hostility and violence. Several satanism-obsessed young people have murdered one or both parents.

Satanist cults encourage fear, hatred, and rejection of society, thereby aggravating members' alienation instead of diminishing it. Some cults advocate anarchy, chaos, and the destruction of all authority, and encourage criminal and antisocial acts.

Members believe they are acquiring power, but in reality they are being stripped of their free will and control of their lives through fear, delusions, drug abuse, violence, vulnerability to blackmail, and criminal acts. Lower-level members may be virtually enslaved by powerful leaders through fear, delusions of power, and consequences of illegal activities.

In most satanist cults, the emphasis on hate, violence, and power over others tends to inhibit positive, gentler feelings that contribute to intimacy. Members may experience a reduced capacity to form close human relationships outside the cult.

Physical deterioration is frequently reported, especially when drug or alcohol abuse in involved. Psychotic breaks, self-mutilation, hallucinations, panic attacks, guilt, identity diffusion, paranoia, and suicide attempts--successful and otherwise--are among the problems seen in individuals involved with satanism.

Most satanist cults favor extreme rejection of personal and mainstream cultural values in favor of satanist values stressing power over others, aggression, hedonism, sexual conquests, and greed for unearned wealth. Members may be required to formalize the break with their pasts by signing a pact with Satan in their own blood and/or committing a criminal act.

In the community at large, violence-prone satanist cults contribute to problems such as vandalism, truancy, and cruelty to animals, as well as to more serious crimes such as arson, drug and alcohol abuse, child abuse and molestation, pornography, drug trafficking, blackmail, theft, and murder. Obsession with satanism accounts for at least some of the increase in teen suicides. In addition, some satanist cults harass, intimidate, threaten and/or terrorize critics, investigators, members, and former members, as well as their families and professionals who come to their aid. Many satanist cult members and ex-members say that they have been threatened with death if they leave and/or speak out against the cult. In addition to the victims themselves, attorneys handling cult-related cases, reporters investigating satanism-related stories, and mental-health professionals who counsel satanist cult survivors have reported being harassed and threatened.

Signs of Involvement

Following are signs of possible adolescent involvement in satanism. It is important not to jump to conclusions. Many of the signs such as heavy alcohol or drug use, in and of themselves, have nothing to do with satanism and may be associated with many other types of problems such as drug addiction and depression. Parents and helping professionals, then, must look at the whole picture. Moreover, they should keep in mind that destructive satanic involvement will often be associated with, if not in fact result from, more traditional psychological problems such as low self-esteem, depression, alienation, etc. The helpers' actions, therefore, ought not to focus solely on the satanic aspect of the person's behavior. Attention must also be paid to problems that predate, exacerbate, cause, or result from the satanic behavior.

Signs of satanic involvement noted by researchers include:

1. Accumulating satanic paraphernalia, such as books (*Satanic Bible, Satanic Rituals, Necronomicon*, books about Satan, witchcraft, the occult, etc.), knives and other weapons, whips, black or red candles and robes, bones, posters depicting sex, violence, or satanist/occult images. Symbols such as inverted pentagrams (five-pointed star with one point facing downwards) or upside-down crosses, the number "666" or the letters "FFF" (sixth letter of the alphabet), the swastika, snakes, spiders. Graffiti such as "DW" (Devil Worship), "Natas" (Satan spelled backwards), "Nema" (Amen spelled backwards), "Redrum" (Murder spelled backwards), "Live" (Evil spelled backwards), or "Satan rules." Drawings of skulls, devil faces or demons, monsters, goat's heads, knives or daggers dripping blood, scenes of violence or mutilation, especially if done in blood. Any of these slogans or symbols used in tattoos or other body markings. Some teens have actually set up satanic altars in their bedrooms, complete with candles, incense, skulls, ritual knives, and satanic symbols.

2. Use of satanic signs and symbols in jewelry, sewn on clothing, or drawn on papers, books, or walls. Sometimes the satanic symbols are written, scratched, or tattooed on the body as the person becomes more deeply involved. One fingernail may be painted black. Satanists may signal each other with "the devil's horns"--a closed fist with the index and little fingers raised--although this is often done just to emulate rock stars who use it. Some teenagers who adopt these symbols may also be involved with variations on the "energy vampire" philosophy, which teaches that you can gain power by sapping energy from others.

3. Developing an obsession with movies, videos, books, and heavy-metal music with themes of occultism and demonism, violence, rape, mutilation, suicide, and death; obsession with fantasy role-playing games; obsession with ouija boards and/or tarot cards and means of predicting the future. [Note: While a young person's interest in the occult, heavy-metal music, fantasy role-playing games, and/or horror movies should be monitored carefully, evidence of a peripheral interest does not necessarily mean that he/she will become heavily involved in satanism or the occult.]

4. Displaying signs of ritualistic mutilation such as unexplained cuts on the left arm or chest area, especially if these are in the form of occult symbols; tattoos (which may be of the homemade variety), excessive piercing of ears or other parts of the body.

5. Erratic grades, falling grades, loss of interest in schoolwork.

6. Serious misbehavior, such as vandalism, theft, arson, cruelty to animals, chronic truancy, running away from home, graverobbing, breaking and entering.

7. Maintaining a "book of shadows," which is a notebook in which rituals and other activities are recorded.

8. Extreme changes in the youth's personality, such as mood swings, humorlessness, aggressiveness, sullenness, secretiveness, or extreme arrogance.

9. Preoccupation with death, particularly the morbid side of it. This may be expressed verbally or through dress, drawings, poetry, or music.

10. Any hints that the youth may be thinking about suicide, such as giving away possessions, withdrawing from friends and family, talking about suicide.

11. Making a pact to sell one's soul to Satan in return for power, money, fame, and success; making a pact promising to commit suicide at a given date; suicide pacts among members of a cult.

12. Adopting unusual nicknames, especially if related to the occult, horror movies, fantasy role-playing games, and the like.

13. Any hints that the youngster believes he/she is possessed by demons.

14 Avoiding family members; expressing extreme hostility towards family's religious beliefs. Aggression towards family, teachers, police, clergy, and other authority figures.

15. Expressing extreme aversion to Christianity and other non-satanic religions.

16. Dropping old friends and activities; secretiveness about new friends and activities.

17. Unexplained disappearances, especially at night. Some teenagers have been known to sneak out in the middle of the night to attend rituals.

18. Making references to drinking blood; hoarding containers of blood or animal parts, sometimes in the back of the family refrigerator.

19. Heavy alcohol or drug use, when accompanied by other symptoms.

20. Expressing racist, anti-Semitic, or white-supremacist attitudes.

References

Bourget,D., Gagnon, A. and Bradford, J.M.W. (1988). Satanism in a psychiatric adolescent population. *Canadian Journal of Psychiatry*, 33.

Freedman, D.X. (1986). Psychiatric epidemiology counts. *Archives of General Psychiatry*, 41, 931-933.

Gallant, Sandi. (January 4, 1990). Personal communication with Dr. Michael Langone.

Gallup Youth Survey Release. (October 26, 1988; March 22, 1989; May 10, 1989).

Markowitz, A. (1989, October). Presentation at Cult Awareness Network Conference, Teaneck, NJ.

Murphy, K. and Zilliox, L. (1989, October). Satanism. Presentations given at Cult Awareness Network National Conference, Teaneck, NJ, October 1989.

Pulling, P. (1989). *The Devil's Web*. Lafayette, LA: Huntington House, Inc.

Scott, G.G. (1984). *The Magicians: A Study of the Use of Power in a Black Magic Group*. Oakland, CA: Creative Communications.

Tucker, R. Teen Satanism. Paper presented at Ritual Abuse: Fact or

Fiction? Conference sponsored by The Institute for the Prevention of Child Abuse, Aylmer, Ontario (May 29-30, 1989).

Wheeler, B.R., Wood, S. and Hatch, J.R. (1988, November-December). Assessment and intervention with adolescents involved in satanism. *Social Work.*

Cults on Campus: Policy and Legal Issues

The Involvement of College Students in Totalistic Groups: Causes, Concerns, Legal Issues, and Policy Considerations

Gregory S. Blimling, Ph.D.

Religious activities on college campuses grew throughout the decade of the 1980's. By 1984, students were clamoring for more religious classes at public universities, and were joining and attending religious services in record numbers (Newsweek, 1984). Boyer (1987), president of the Carnegie Foundation for the Advancement of Teaching, confirmed this continuing interest in religion, observing that "religious groups are among the fastest-growing organizations on many campuses" (p. 187). He notes further that the charismatic and revival groups have seen a particular increase, while mainstream Protestant groups have a "rather small following among undergraduates." (p. 188) National surveys of incoming college freshmen indicate that 5.6% of new college freshmen in 1985 indicated that their religious preferences fell outside of traditional religious organizations (Austin, 1986). The increase in religious activity, and the often controversial behavior of nontraditional, fundamentalist, and cult religious groups on college campuses, has been an issue of concern among college administrators (Biemiller, 1983). This article addresses these issues as they apply to college campuses.

The article is organized into four sections. The first section explores why college students are particularly susceptible to cult involvement. In the second section, cult recruiting on campus is examined, and the problems associated with cult involvement are reviewed in the third section. The article concludes with an examination of legal issues and policy considerations which educational administrators need to consider in working with cult groups and with students cults are attempting to recruit.

The term "cult" is used throughout this chapter to refer to a totalist religious group which dominates members' attention and rigidly prescribes their conduct in most of their daily activities. These groups are customarily associated with a living, highly charismatic leader (Whittier, 1979), tend to have a preoccupation with the attainment of money (Lynn, 1979), and frequently employ coercive and deceptive techniques to recruit and convert new members (Shapiro, 1977). A principle feature of many cult groups is that they isolate their members from their families of origin, and often from the rest of society, except where such association serves the interest of the cult: fund-raising. Although the concept of a "religion" is implicit in the definition of a cult as it is used here, this formal designation is not a prerequisite. Some highly dogmatic, pseudo-psychotherapy groups may, without formal association, serve the same spiritual functions as a religion.

Susceptibility of College Students to Cult Involvement

It is probably true that anyone, given the right set of circumstances, can be converted to membership in a religious cult. What is not as apparent is why some people are drawn to these groups while others are able to remain independent. One of the methods for discovering why people join is to ask the question, "Who joins?" Research has shown (Galanter, 1979; Clark, 1976) that over half of all new members are in the adult transitional years--between 18 and 24 years old. It is not by coincidence that many cult groups focus on this age period. They recognize that young adults in search of identity are vulnerable, easily deceived, and filled with a certain naive idealism which can be used by cults to win new converts.

The common theme of the adult transitional years is the search and integration for identity. Erickson (1968) was among the first to recognize the importance of this period, 18-24, as a time which one devotes to establishing identity. The critical stages he observed in this period are the interplay between the need for intimacy with others versus isolation and the recognition of a self-identity versus role confusion. Resolution of these issues involves (1) experimenting with various roles and lifestyles, (2) having the freedom to choose activities and experience the consequence of those choices, (3) feeling involved in what can be seen as meaningful achievement, and (4) having time for introspection and reflection.

Other researchers (Sanford, 1967; Coons, 1974; Havighurst, 1953) have elaborated upon Erikson's observations of the developmental stages leading to adulthood. These theories of psychological development offer insight into why young adults in the transitional years between childhood and adulthood are so susceptible to the intrusive proselytizing and coercive persuasion of cult groups. An examination of each of these theories exceeds the scope of this chapter and is unnecessary to illustrate why, in this period of transition, young adults are so vulnerable. Instead, one theory, that of Chickering (1972), will be used to illustrate why college students, and others in this developmental period, are so psychologically susceptible to cult involvement.

Psychosocial Development: Chickering's Theory

Briefly, Chickering hypothesizes seven vectors of development which begin in childhood and continue throughout a person's life. The first three of these vectors form a framework for the establishment of a self-concept. They consist of (1) establishing intellectual, physical, and social competence, (2) learning to recognize and manage emotions, and (3) developing autonomy. These three developmental vectors are issues principal to the normal psychological maturation of students in the freshman and sophomore years. It is the integration of these three vectors which forms the initial stages of an adult ego identity, which Chickering considers to be the fourth vector of development. This fourth vector, identity, serves as the framework for the resolution of the last three vectors: (5) freeing of interpersonal relationships, (6) establishing purpose, and (7) developing integrity. These latter three vectors are developmental concerns of the junior year of college and beyond. All seven vectors continue throughout life, and form other developmental issues in later-life transitions (Levinson, 1978; Kegan, 1982).

Any of these seven vectors can serve as the basis for unresolved crises in which a student may seek to escape the crises by joining a cult. As one example, consider the vector of autonomy. It is comprised of two competing issues: emotional independence and instrumental independence. Emotional independence is characterized by college students in their struggle to break the parent-child relationship and exchange it for an adult-to-adult relationship. This is inhibited in college students by the financial ties they have with their parents, who usually assume all or at least part of the cost for their college expenses. Lacking the instrumental autonomy of financial independence inhibits the freeing of the parental bonds of control and accountability. Cult groups offer one form of resolving this struggle for autonomy. Instrumentally, they offer students financial independence from parents in exchange for financial dependence on the cult group. Emotionally, they offer the student a physical break with the control and accountability to parents, which they exchange for the illusion of personal autonomy in the cult.

Even after students have established a formative identity, they remain vulnerable. As students struggle to free their interpersonal relationships, they take greater risks in self-disclosure and intimacy. General friendships are replaced by more intimate ones, usually focusing on a significant other person. Again, when students are confronted with difficulty in establishing these more meaningful levels of emotional intimacy with others, cults are there to offer a replacement with their psychological techniques of "love bombing" and communal surrogate family structures. These help the student resolve the immediate crises, but offer only a temporary and superficial resolution in exchange for the person's obedience to the cult.

Cognitive Development: Perry's Theory

Although cults recruit principally by attacking people psychologically and not intellectually, the cognitive stage of students' development may predispose them to a cult's message. Perry (1970), in his study of college students, has suggested that students enter college as dualistic reasoners and move to an acceptance of pluralistic reasons and finally into a state of relativistic reasoning. Freshmen commonly believe that there are absolute rights and wrongs and that these truths are known to those in positions of authority, such as college professors. The process of education moves students from this dualistic reasoning to an acceptance of pluralistic truths, and finally into various forms of relativistic reasoning in which one sees truth in the context of experience, evidence, credibility, and values. When students are confronted by ideas which cannot be explained using the cognitive reasoning to which they are accustomed, they begin a process of adapting to a new form of reasoning, or they escape the process of development by rigidly adhering to their current form of reasoning, or they regress to a less complex stage of reasoning. Confronted by an uncertain world in which truths are relative, some students seek the sanctuary of a cult group, which absolves them of decision-making and supplies them with a complete set of absolute truths derived from the dogma of the cult. Acceptance, by faith, alleviates the dissonance created by the uncertainties of the world of relativism and offers a reassuring, albeit naive, reality.

Moral Development: Kohlberg's Theory

Another psychological area in which college students are particularly vulnerable to cult involvement concerns the progress of their moral development. Kohlberg (1981) explains moral development as a six-stage progression from beliefs based on egocentric reasoning to those based on sociocentric reasoning, to those based on alleocentric reasoning. Students enter college at either stage three or stage four in Kohlberg's moral stage development scheme. Both of these stages employ sociocentric reasoning. In stage-three moral reasoning, students are concerned with self as a member of the peer group. What is right is determined by peer approval. In stage-four reasoning, students are concerned with the self as a member of society. What is right is defined by obeying the rules of the social order. Anywhere in this process of moral growth the cults can intervene. At stage-three reasoning, the appeal is the communal nature of the group and the peer support it offers. At stage-four reasoning, the appeal of the cult is for the alleged worthiness of their organization--the greater good of the world--and the absolute laws which guide the cult's dogma.

The transition to college can be a very threatening experience for many students. Often it is the first time that students have been absent from the family of origin for a prolonged time. The identity which has sustained them throughout high school is shed as they enter college, where what one did in high school is seen as a link with the past and is of little interest to the other college students. Most students make this transition with only the normal adjustment anxiety and uncertainty that accompany any such life change. Other students find this experience to be much more threatening and frequently seek easy solutions to complex social adjustment problems.

Because the college years are a period of transition and uncertainty, students are particularly vulnerable to the psychological persuasion of cults. Psychosocially, students are struggling with adapting to new adult roles. Cognitively, students are learning more complex ways to reason while relinquishing the safety and security of the adolescent and preadolescent years. And morally, students' beliefs are being challenged to grow from the dependability and direct feedback received from peers and family members to a reliance on the larger social structure of society. These changes, although not restricted to this age period of 18-24, are perhaps most dynamic during this period because these life changes represent a move from the nuclear family to independence.

Social Factors

Another way to ask the question about why students are joining cults is to ask, "Why are they joining *now*?" Is there something about contemporary society which makes cults a more compelling option for students in the world today than in the past? Toffler (1971) suggested that there are so many choices students must make in college that they may be confronted by what he called "over choice." One resolution to this "over choice" in today's society is to stop making the choices for oneself and let others do it for you. Coons (1974) suggests that this is one of the appeals of cults. These groups offer an escape from self-determination by absolving individuals from having to reason for themselves. This is replaced with the decisions cults make for individuals as revealed through the groups' dogmas.

Cox (1977) suggests that society today has failed to fulfill the basic human need to belong and have the support of the community. As institutions have become more egalitarian, larger, and the faculty more specialized and compartmentalized, the sense of community on many college campuses has been lost. Boyer (1987), in a report by the Carnegie Foundation on the status of American undergraduate education, notes that "almost two out of five of today's undergraduates still say they do not feel a sense of community at their institution (p. 191)."

In an earlier report by the Carnegie Foundation, Levine (1980) suggested that one reason for this lack of community is that students have lost faith in higher education and in other social institutions such as the church, the family, and the government because these institutions have failed to meet their ideals. He observed that students were either abandoning traditional religions or were seeking new religions. Levine explains this seeming paradox in this way: "When faith or interest in traditional religions decline, new religions are a common development, particularly when trust in normally-competing social institutions is low. To a subgroup of young people looking for something to believe in, non-traditional religions with an emphasis on community or a well-defined dogma for guidance have been particularly appealing" (pp. 98-99).

The combination of students in the midst of confronting the normal developmental issues leading to adulthood, college environments which are larger and less supportive to students, and the stress of being presented lifestyle options not afforded previous generations, helps to make college students particularly vulnerable to the recruiting practices of cults. Given this combination of circumstances, cults find a fertile territory when they come to college campuses seeking students to recruit and convert.

Cult Recruitment of College Students

College campuses contain high percentages of upper-middle-class white students who are confronting the normal transitional issues leading to adulthood. Students generally have unscheduled leisure time and the opportunity to experiment with different lifestyle options as a method for determining what suits them. They also possess the youthful enthusiasm and ideological commitments which become more difficult to sustain as one grows older and makes other life commitments.

The proliferation of cult groups on college campuses has been extensive. At the University of California - Berkeley, for example, it is estimated that at least 200 different religious sects on and off-campus are recruiting from the 30,000-student campus (Anderson, 1981).

Types of Recruiting

There are two kinds of recruiters which haunt college campuses. The first is the trained cult leader sent to a campus for the purpose of establishing a group. The second type is the zealous new member eager to share his/her experience in much the same way as a recently-sobered alcoholic has the need to share his/her change in lifestyle. Recruiters are taught to look for students who are confronting transitional life experiences, who are depressed, or who are under stress or in crisis. Because conversion to a cult is an attack on one's emotions and not one's intellect, recruiters have the greatest advantage when students are most vulnerable. Freshmen and seniors are sometimes specifically targeted, because both are in the midst of major life-transitional experiences.

Any campus location can provide an opportunity for the cult recruiter to make an initial contact. Recruiters have been known to station themselves at university counseling centers to find students who are emotionally vulnerable (Enroth, 1979), wander the corridors of the residence halls to find students who are feeling lonely (Stoehr, 1978), and to loiter about college libraries looking for students whose reading topics might offer an opportunity to initiate a discussion that could lead to a continuing relationship (Bromley & Shupe, 1979). Students who have recently ended a relationship with a boyfriend or a girlfriend make particularly good prospects. An attractive male or female student can befriend the recently-jilted student for the purpose of gaining a new recruit.

One must remember that cult recruiters, both those specifically trained for the purpose and those who are simply zealous new members, are motivated by a commitment to the worthiness of the cult. When they deceive, manipulate, or coerce another person into the steps leading to conversion, they do so with the unshakable belief that they are helping that person to become closer to God or to whatever other principle, deity, or experience they are professing. For the cult recruiter, the ends do justify the means.

Students are not the only ones deceived by cult members. College administrators, the police, or patrons to an event from whom they are seeking donations are all equally "uninformed and naive" and are therefore assumed by cult members to be unable to make decisions based on the full knowledge of the circumstances. Therefore, they reason, deception is justified.

Recruitment Methods

The three methods most commonly used to recruit on campus are (1) casual contact, (2) street corner evangelism, and (3) becoming a student organization. The first of these, casual contacts, was discussed briefly above. It involves canvassing the campus and locating "likely" prospects for the purpose of inviting the student to an initial meeting or weekend retreat. The second form of recruiting is what I have termed "street-corner evangelism," which consists of "soapbox" lectures given by a cult leader. These talks may address some major world crisis or the teachings of the cult. In the first instance, the leader is generally interested in identifying students who are willing to commit themselves to some alleged worthy cause. The recruiter's intent is to get some of the audience to commit to come to some form of organizational meeting or retreat--which in actuality is an intense recruiting program. In the second instance, the recruiter explains the cult's mission and its "benefits" to students. The Bible or "self-help" principles akin to pop-psychology are frequently used as the forum for this discussion. Drawing from what students know about these topics, the recruiter extends or reinterprets passages from the Bible or generally accepted psychological principles as a method for helping students discover something of interest to them so they will attend more serious discussions of the topic.

The third form of recruiting is for a cult group to seek the recognition of the university as a student organization. In becoming a student organization, the cult gains access to university facilities and may gain access to some student funds, forums to recruit students, and university mailing lists of new students. Perhaps most importantly, the cult gains some legitimacy through the recognition procedure. Despite the distance a university might wish to put between itself and the activities of the cult, to students and to the public, university recognition implies some form of acceptance or approval by the university community. Because public universities have limited criteria by which they can deny recognition to groups seeking to affiliate, this recognition may not imply approval, but merely that the group has met the minimum criteria courts have established for recognition.

These three common recruiting methods on college campuses should not be viewed as mutually exclusive, or exhaustive. Other recruiting schemes are certainly available. One with which the author is personally familiar involved an attempt to infiltrate the Resident Assistant staff in several college residence halls. The plan was to have cult members hired as resident assistants and subsequently located in the same residence hall with other members living in the living units supervised by these resident assistants. Gradually, through peer pressure, guilt, and nightly classes held in the floor lounge, members of this organization attempted to recruit the other members of the floor. The plan was then to have these members move to other living units in the same building and continue the process floor by floor until they had converted an entire building. Fortunately, the plan was circumvented in its initial stages by an alert residence hall staff.

One of the major problems college administrators face in working with these groups is discovering who the groups really are. Many practice deception: they are not reluctant to cloak the actual name of the cult by using organizational names not known to the public.

The greatest threat faced by students is not from recruiters exposing their beliefs. College campuses should offer a forum for the exchange of ideas regardless of how unorthodox a set of beliefs might be. The threat to students is the unprincipled, psychologically-coercive behavior which accompanies many of these recruiting efforts. Many students join these groups because of deception. It is these recruiting behaviors which university administrators must restrict.

Problems Associated with Cults on Campus

Unlike many campus religious groups whose mission is to support the spiritual life of students and assist them in their college endeavors, cult groups seek students to assist only the cult organization. As students become drawn into the cult, they are gradually separated from the college until their life is so consumed with the daily requirements of the cult that important academic work goes unattended, or they are moved to another location away from the influence of the college and their friends. The issue here is not retention of students, but the well-being of students. Cult conversion and membership replaces critical thinking with cult jargon, dogmatic adherence to cult doctrine, and creates the inability to reason or think independently (Conway & Siegelman, 1978). This is perhaps cults' greatest threat. It is the antithesis of what colleges and universities have been organized to teach.

There are other documented changes in the personalities of young people who have joined cults. Students' speech and writing lose irony and metaphor, and their vocabulary is reduced, taking on a rote memorized style (Clark, 1979). Intellectually, cult members appear to exhibit a decrease in intelligence and, if they leave the cult, they are frequently forced to assume menial jobs until they can relearn thinking for themselves (Delgado, 1977; Singer, 1979). Other mental harms include reduction of cognitive flexibility and adaptability, narrowing and blunting of affection, regression of behavior to childlike levels, and possible pathological symptoms, including disassociation, delusions, and similar mental disorders (Delgado, 1977).

Even this listing of harms does not capture the devastating impact that such membership has on the emotional life of students and their families. The hopes, aspirations, and dreams of students and their parents are usurped by these groups. Several years ago I met with a former student who left the university for a weekend retreat in New Orleans with a group of students associated with what was at that time a campus organization. He never returned to the university. He was living in Chicago, where he had been sent by the organization shortly after he had become a member. For the first time in almost ten years he was being given "permission" by the leadership to come back and visit his mother.

He told me that after being in a training camp for a while, he had been sent to the Chicago area where he became part of a mobile fund raising team which sold flowers. Apparently he was very good at it--raising between $200 and $300 a day and more than twice this much on certain holidays like Mother's Day. As a trusted member of the organization he was permitted to retain some of the money for the purpose of starting a business which would wholesale fresh fish to oriental restaurants in the Chicago area. He indicated that in the year preceding this visit, the company he started grossed in excess of a million dollars, the profits from which all went to the cult. He was given a subsistence allowance. The money he needed to travel to see his mother was given to him by the cult and he was permitted to stay with her for a week, during which time he was required to check with local members of the cult who would in turn check on him.

Now, at the age of thirty, this person was seeking more in his life. In a mass marriage arranged by the cult leadership, he had been married to a woman from another country. He met her only once prior to the marriage and was denied permission to consummate the marriage until he and his wife brought seven new members into the cult. After the marriage, he returned to Chicago and his wife was sent to Houston to work for the cult. He regretted not having a family, not spending more time with his mother, not being able to buy some things that he would have liked to make his life more comfortable, and he resented being so totally dependent on the cult for his existence. He said he envied some of his high school friends who had careers and families. Despite all of this, he was not prepared to leave the cult. He simply did not know how to leave or what he could do if he left.

This very sensitive and capable person had been led to so devalue himself--even though he had established a very successful business on very little capital--that he believed he owed his very existence to the cult. He lacked the motivation, skills, and self-confidence to leave and to realize the dreams he had for himself.

This is only one of many stories of young people who leave college to join a cult. College administrators seldom hear from them again. These students are lost among the thousands of others who are moving through the universities, changing schools, dropping out, or stopping out for periods of time. As universities have grown larger, they have come to lose sight of the lives of individual students. It is only when the situation becomes acute or a particular student's problem is brought to the attention of the appropriate college administrator that efforts are mounted to address the problem created by the cults. Most of the time they quietly draw students away from colleges without anyone but the parents feeling or knowing of the loss.

Most of the problems cults pose on college campuses are associated with psychological, emotional, and financial harm to individual students and to their families. There are, however, some extremist cult groups which are even more harmful.

One of the recent cult attractions among high school students is an interest in satanism and the occult. During the past several years many newspaper articles (Zorn, 1986; Washington, 1986; Stone, 1986; Man Charged, 1985; Burks, 1986; Satan Worship, 1984; Baird, 1984) have reported on homicides, suicides, and animal sacrifices involving adolescents who were associated with some form of satanic cult. One of the links between satanism and its new interest among some young people appears to be heavy-metal rock music. A folklore surrounding some of the popular heavy-metal rock music groups suggest that some groups are "devil worshipers."

Reports of satanic cults have surfaced in places such as Chicago, Albuquerque, El Paso, Oklahoma City, and Logan, Ohio. It is difficult to know how prevalent these groups are because they are very secretive. One estimate is that out of the 3,500 or so cult groups functioning in the United States, about 500 are associated with the occult (Baird, 1984). How many are violent is not known. Concern about satanic groups resolves around existence of ritual deaths, animal and human sacrifices, and other acts of violence. Clearly, participation in one of these extremist groups presents a threat to the individuals in the group and in many cases to the community in which the group operates.

Although college campuses have not been associated with any of the more public reports of satanic group activity, a number of high school students have (cf. Langone & Blood, 1990). It is reasonable to assume that some high school students have continued these associations in college; indeed, the presence of satanic graffiti (e.g., inverted crosses, the number 666 indicating the sign of the devil, pentagrams) on buildings on or near the college campus and students who have tattooed themselves with similar symbols suggest that, as with other segments of society, satanic groups are probably functioning on college campuses.

Legal Considerations in Working with Cults on Campus

University administrators have no legitimate interest in controlling the content of a religious belief. The freedom to hold a belief, however, is separate from the freedom to act upon that belief. It is here that university administrators have an interest in controlling cult behaviors that threaten the well-being of students. The courts have provided guidelines for university administrators working with the complex issues associated with religious cults and First Amendment rights.

The plethora of legal issues surrounding the free expression of religious beliefs, the establishment of religion, the rights of association, and freedom of speech make working with cult groups a complex issue at public universities. Private colleges which are not significantly involved in state action--meaning that they are not so intertwined in the public sector as to make the college indistinguishable from public institutions--have greater latitude in working with these groups. There is no requirement that private colleges consider these groups for recognition. They have the legal right to restrict cult leaders from being on their campuses, except where these leaders have become students.

College administrators must grapple with managing the intrusive proselytizing of cult groups and determining what involvement, if any, they are to have on campus. Four issues must be considered: a) legal implications, b) the development of institutional policies to control the behavior of these groups, c) identification of pro-active educational measures that will inform and prepare students for the recruiting efforts of these groups, and d) consideration of how one works with existing on-campus groups and future groups which become part of the campus community. Subsequent sections will deal with each of these issues.

The days when college administrators could operate in *loco parentis* for students have long since passed. They have been replaced by court decisions which form the framework for much administrative decision-making in today's litigious society.

Although the courts have occasionally strayed into the issue of religion at private colleges, for the most part, the issue of religious freedom has been one adjudicated principally at institutions of public higher education. These challenges have been set in the context of the religion clauses of the First Amendment. Embodied in these religion clauses are three concepts: religion, the establishment of religion, and religious expression. Chief Justice Burger, writing for the Court in *Lemon v. Kurtzman* 403 U.S. 602 (1971), observed of these clauses that the language was "at best opaque, particularly when compared with other portions of the Amendment" (p. 612). The language and fluctuating interpretations of religion have caused confusion at public universities, which have attempted to balance the religious liberty rights of students with the duty of the university as a state agency to maintain a separation between church and state. Most of the conflicts between students and public universities have focused on: (1) use of facilities by religious organizations, (2) religious proselytizing, (3) religious conduct, and (4) recognition of student organizations.

Use of Facilities by Student Religious Organizations

The question of whether or not permitting students to use university facilities for religious purposes violates the establishment clause of the First Amendment was raised in *Keegan v. University of Delaware*, 349 A. 2d 14 (Del., 1975) when a group of Roman Catholic students requested the use of one of the public areas of the University-owned residence hall for the purpose of holding regular religious services. The University of Delaware had a policy which prohibited the use of its facilities for any religious purpose under the belief that such support would violate the establishment clause. The Supreme Court of Delaware overturned a lower court ruling to find on behalf of the students, striking down the University's policy. In doing so, the Court concluded that because no religious group would be given special accommodation by a change in the University's policy--and if there was, such benefit would be incidental--there was no infringement of the establishment clause.

In *Chess v. Widman*, 480 F.Supp 907 (W.D. MO., 1979), the University of Missouri - Kansas City denied the use of its facilities for regular religious service to a fundamentalist Christian student organization on the premise that the Supreme Court's interpretation of the Higher Education Facilities Act of 1963 in *Tilton v. Richardson* 403 U.S.672 (1970) prohibited the sectarian use of any college or university facility built under the provisions of this act. The court held that by letting the fundamentalist Christian organization, called Cornerstone, regularly use University facilities the University would be advancing religion in violation of the establishment clause. In reaching its decision supporting the University, the Court specifically disagreed with the Delaware Supreme Court in *Keegan v. University of Delaware*.

However, on appeal (635 F.2d 1310, {App. Ct. 8th Cir., 1980}), the decision of the *Chess v. Widman* court was reversed. In upholding the right of the student organization to use University facilities for regular religious meetings, the Appellate Court found that the University could not deny equal access to a public forum on the basis of the content of the message, religious, political, or otherwise. The University of Missouri-Kansas City appealed to the U.S. Supreme Court (*Widmar v. Vincent*, 454 U.S. 263 {1981}), which affirmed the Appellate Court's ruling.

It is probably safe to conclude that public universities can permit students to use facilities for religious purposes without violating the establishment clause. Denying the use of university facilities to religious groups when the facilities are made available to other campus organizations has been considered by the courts to be an unfair restriction on students' free expression rights under the First Amendment.

Religious Proselytizing

The courts have recognized individuals' rights to express their religious beliefs, even when that expression may be an annoyance to others (*Douglas v. City of Jeannette*, 1943). The free expression of belief--which may include the distribution of literature or the sale of religious material--is considered in light of the sincerity of the held belief and a compelling state interest in controlling that belief. The case of the *International Society of Krishna Consciousness (ISKCON) v. Barber* 650 F.2d 430 (2nd Cir., 1981) serves to demonstrate the extent to which the courts will go to permit the free expression of religious belief. In *ISKON v. Barber*, officials of the New York State Fair attempted to control the "begging" and proselytizing of ISKCON by restricting and ultimately barring the solicitation of money and proselytizing activities by any group on the fair grounds. ISKON sued, contending that the regulation placed an unfair restriction on their Sankirtan belief. Although the defendants were able to show numerous examples of fraud, street scams, quick money change deals, deception and other unlawful acts which ISKCON devotees had been trained to use to acquire money from patrons under the guise of religious proselytizing, the U.S. Court of Appeals, striking down a lower court ruling, declared that, "Notwithstanding evidence that fraud is occasionally involved in the practice of Sankirtan, the state has failed to show that methods less restrictive than outright prohibition are ineffective in checking misconduct. Accordingly, we hold that the state unconstitutionally interfered with the free exercise rights of ISKCON members by enacting and enforcing its anti-solicitation rule" (*ISKCON v. Barber, 1981*).

University campuses, however, are "not open to the public in the same way that streets and parks are" (*Widman v. Vincent,* 1981, p. 278). Universities do have the right to control time, place, and manner (*Healy v. James,* 1972) of religious proselytizing, meetings, distribution of printed material, and to exercise similar control over the environs of its campus--provided that the restrictions are reasonable and applied consistently to religious and non-religious groups alike.

Ohio State University attempted to control the distribution of a fundamentalist Christian newspaper called *Today's Student* by controlling the time, place, and manner of distribution. Although restrictions placed on distribution of this material were similar to those imposed on other University groups, they were different from the wider distribution of the University supported newspaper, *The Lantern.* The Solid Rock Foundation, the campus group wishing to distribute the newspaper, sought a restraining order to prohibit the University from interfering with its free exercise rights under the First Amendment (*Solid Rock Foundation v. The Ohio State University,* 478 F.Supp.96. {S.D. Ohio, E.D., 1979}). The University argued that such wide distribution would violate the establishment clause by excessively entangling the University in the dissemination of religious material. The Court disagreed with the University's contention and found that although the University had controlled only time, place, and manner, the restrictions were unreasonable in that it did not allow the student organization to reach all segments of the student population and, therefore, abridged the students' free exercise rights.

Non-student groups may have limited rights on state university campuses. These rights include the dissemination of free printed material, the freedom to engage a passer-by in religious or political discussions, and the freedom to speak at forums open to the public. Conversely, non-student groups do not have the right to sell publications, food, or other items, nor to engage in other forms of fund-raising without the permission of the university. The Court in *Glover v. Cole*, 762 F.2d. 1197, U.S. Appellate Court (4th Ct.), 1985 acknowledged this when it held that West Virginia State College could regulate the manner in which third parties used University property differently than the manner afforded student groups.

The issue of religious proselytizing on campus was also addressed in *Chapman v. Thomas*, ...F.Supp..., No. 80-757-CIV-5, (U.S. Dist. Ct., E.E., NC, Raleigh Div., 1982). North Carolina State University had a policy which restricted door-to-door solicitation in University residence halls. The policy was challenged by Scott Chapman (a student) after he received a university disciplinary sanction for violating this policy in his attempt to promote his Christian beliefs by conducting door-to-door evangelism in a University residence hall. The Court upheld the University's policy. In ruling for the university, the Court found that the residence halls were not a public forum, but were similar to one's household. So long as the University uniformly enforced the non-solicitation policy, the Court supported the University restriction as a permissible infringement on the religious liberty rights of Mr. Chapman.

It can be concluded from this analysis that universities may reasonably control time, place, and manner of religious proselytizing on campus in areas considered public forums, consistent with its regulation of other groups. Universities may restrict door-to-door evangelism (at least in the Federal District of Raleigh N.C., but probably elsewhere) where it also restricts other forms of door-to-door solicitation.

Religious Conduct

Although the courts have protected religious proselytizing in most forums, it has not protected all forms of religious conduct. It has been established that the freedom to hold beliefs is legally separate from the freedom to act on those beliefs when the state has a compelling interest in doing so (Wood, 1979).

Students have on occasion attempted to assert their right to use drugs under the guise of religious expression. Although the U.S. Supreme Court did let stand a unique interpretation by the California Supreme Court in People v. Woody 61 Cal. 2d 716, 394 P.2d 813, (1964), which held that the use of peyote by Navaho Indians who were members of the Native American Church was a religious sacrament under the protection of the First Amendment free-exercise clause, the use of drugs for alleged religious reasons has generally not been sustained by the courts.

It is probably fair to say that universities are not compelled to permit students unrestricted license for insidious, unlawful, or hedonistic conduct under the assertion of religious liberty. Nevertheless, the university may not seek to control religious conduct solely because it believes the conduct to be abhorrent.

Recognition of Religious Student Organizations

Where public universities recognize or register organizations, the free exercise of religion also extends to the right of students to organize for the purpose of advancing common purposes through a student organization. If a university recognizes or registers any student organization, it must use the same set of nondiscriminatory policies in considering the application of all student organizations, whether they be for a secular, political, social, academic, or other lawful purpose.

The issue of student organizations and their right to affiliate at public universities has been an issue of court interest in its own right. In the landmark case of *Healy v. James*, 408 U.S. 169 (1972), the Supreme Court held that Central Connecticut State College could not deny recognition to a local chapter of the Students for a Democratic Society solely on the belief that the organization might do harm. The court established a three-pronged test for nonrecognition as follows: (1) a group advocating lawless action and having the means to carry it out, (2) a group's refusal to follow the reasonable rules and regulations of the university or the law, or (3) a group engaging in any acts that disrupted the university or acts that were unlawful.

In *Aman v. Handler*, 653 F.2d, 41 (1981), the Collegiate Association for the Research of Principles (CARP), one of the front groups used by Rev. Moon's Unification Church to recruit college students into his organization (Hassan, 1981), sought a restraining order against the University of New Hampshire after the group's application for formal recognition was denied by the Vice President for Student Affairs.

Cathy Aman, the plaintiff, alleged that denial of official recognition of CARP by the University of New Hampshire impaired her freedom of religious expression, assembly, and association. A three-judge panel, sitting on appeal, held that the University "failed to meet its burden of showing that it had reasonable grounds for refusing to give recognition to the organization" (*Aman v. Handler*, 1981, p. 41) and remanded the case to the district court--with instructions that the district court decide the case in accordance with the standards established in Healy v. James.

The courts have jealously protected the rights of citizens to freely exercise their religious beliefs. Only where there have been a compelling state interest and a lack of less restrictive means of control have the courts sought to regulate the free expression of religion. In conflicts arising between an individual's free-exercise rights and the interests of public universities to maintain a separation between Church and State, the courts generally have ruled in ways that provide the greatest religious liberty to the individual.

Universities have yet to demonstrate to the courts compelling reasons of sufficient merit to restrain cults and other totalist religious groups from involvement on campus, even where it can be established that they are psychologically destructive to individuals. Although these groups may represent beliefs that are antithetical to the educational mission of an institution and the associated legal conduct is abhorrent to the educational community, the courts have not attempted to intervene to control the lawful exercise of religious belief.

Public university administrators may conclude the following:

1. Public educational facilities may be used by student religious groups.

2. Student religious groups have a right to proselytize on campus (except in the private areas of a university residence hall).

3. Religious conduct which does not violate the law or lawful university policies should be permitted.

4. Where the university recognizes student organizations, religious organizations must also be recognized without regard for their espoused religious beliefs.

5. Policies formulated to regulate student behavior on campus may be applied to religious groups in the same manner as other organizations; however, no special policies which may be construed as defining a suspect religious classification may be enacted to control religious groups.

6. Nonstudent groups have limited rights, which include distributing free literature, engaging people in conversations on any topic, and speaking

at open public forums, but do not necessarily include the right to use university facilities or to conduct fund raising activities on the campus of a state university.

Administrative Policies

Few college administrators are willing to confront the myriad of legal problems one assumes when attempting to restrict cult groups from any involvement on campus. Thus, administrators are left to develop impartial institutional policies designed to control the deceptive and coercive behavior used by many cult groups. This author has argued elsewhere (Blimling, 1981, 1987) that universities should:

1. Require all groups to state clearly the name of the organization and all of its affiliations on all the literature it distributes and in all of the proselytizing it does. (All written material distributed by student organizations must list all affiliations and associations a student organization has with any organization outside of the institution. Advertisements, regardless of the media used, must clearly state the student organization's affiliations as presented in its original application for recognitions or as researched by the university);

2. Develop a policy which prohibits the use of harassment, mind-control techniques, threats, or coercive persuasion to recruit or retain members in any student organization;

3. Restrict door-to-door solicitation in the residence halls and fraternity and sorority houses; and

4. Prohibit student organizations from interfering with or disrupting the lawful educational process, purposes, and functions of the university.

These four policies should be applied to all campus groups and not just to cult groups. However, these policies, if enforced, are likely to have the greatest influence on controlling the behavior of the cult groups who are known to use techniques and approaches in conflict with these policies.

Another approach to this issue has been to establish an "ethical code" for campus evangelism. Reverend Robert Watts Thornburg (ICEP, 1988) at Boston University and others have developed guidelines for ethical behavior by campus religious groups. Their code of ethics restricts behaviors that depersonalize, coerce, manipulate, or attempt to bypass a person's critical faculties. It establishes a commitment to fairness and principles for working with students.

There are other policies which are useful in working with campus groups. Most universities require that a new student organization have a minimum number of full-time students petitioning for recognition before recognition will be considered (e.g., charter membership to be comprised of not less than ten full-time students). This membership requirement does two things. First, it ensures that there is sufficient interest in the formation of a new student organization to merit its recognition, and second, it makes it more difficult for cult groups to register one or two recruiters as students for the purpose of starting a new student organization.

Requiring student organizations to have a faculty sponsor as part of their application for recognition is another policy which has merit. Student organizations should advance the educational mission of the university and contribute to the overall educational experience of students. Faculty, serving in advisory roles with student organizations, can help ensure that these organizations meet these expectations. If interested and actively involved, faculty should be of benefit to students as role models, confidants, and mentors. It is likely that some of the more extreme cult groups will find it difficult to locate a faculty sponsor willing to support its efforts. This faculty sponsorship requirement has the effect of setting a minimum standard for acceptance--namely, that at least one member of the faculty must deem the organization to have educational merit before it can be recognized as a student organization.

Universities can restrict membership in recognized student organizations to students. There is no requirement that universities make their facilities available to individuals who are not members of the university community. This restriction is consistent with the institution's purpose of providing an educational experience for its students, and it helps to control the influence of those over whom the university has no direct control.

Implicit in establishing reasonable rules for the recognition of student organizations and their subsequent conduct is the need to establish a fair procedure to address withdrawing recognition. Most institutions have some form of disciplinary penalties which can be assigned to student organizations which violate the reasonable regulations of the institutions, and these have been successfully applied to religious groups on college campuses (The Collegiate Advisor, 1983). It is appropriate for administrators to reexamine these policies to consider if the due process requirements outlined could be strengthened or clarified. If it becomes necessary to take disciplinary action against one of these campus-affiliated cult groups, it is possible that the matter will be brought to the attention of the courts. The courts will be principally interested in whether or not the student organization was given substantive and procedural due process in any decision reached in holding the organization accountable for the violation of policy.

Private colleges and universities have greater latitude in the recognition of student organizations and in who gets to use their institutional facilities. Colleges which have a recognized religious heritage generally are not compelled to permit the involvement of student organizations which espouse beliefs and values antithetical to the institution's mission. They can justifiably refuse to entertain the cadre of religiously aligned groups wishing to use their campus as a base for recruiting students.

Although these colleges may be insulated against direct campus recruiting through student organizations, they may find these groups establishing organizations on property adjacent to the campus. They may discover cult recruiters haunting places on and off campus where students spend their leisure time, and they may find newly-converted students in the college acting as recruiters for off-campus organizations. Private college administrators need to be sensitive to what they can do with their students and to educational programs they may wish to develop to better inform their students.

Having addressed the issue of cults becoming student organizations through a recognition procedure, the question must also be asked if there is any way for institutions to avoid this level of involvement. Many times these groups are looking only for a public forum to share their beliefs. When institutions have rigidly structured their policies to limit access to the student population, they may be forcing some organizations to become more involved than is perhaps necessary or desirable. If the institution does not currently have an open forum area of the campus where any person can stand on a "soap box" and espouse any belief he or she wishes, it may wish to consider developing this option. When these groups have the latitude to stand and be heard, they offer little threat to anyone. Because cults recruit psychologically and not intellectually, colleges have everything to gain and nothing to lose when these recruiters attempt to explain their synergistic beliefs to a cynical group of often-bemused college students. This public exposure unveils for students the true purposes of these groups and, through the questioning and challenges of the audience, the faulty premises on which the organizations are based. It is when they are forced to conduct their activities covertly that they pose the greatest threat to students.

Educational Programs

One of the most effective means of countering the intrusive proselytizing of cult groups is to inform the student population about the activities of these groups. Many institutions have developed brochures about cult recruiting on campuses, and videotapes, films, and speakers are available through various organizations (e.g., American Family Foundation, International Cult Education Program, Cult Awareness Network) which can be used to inform the general student population.

This educational approach can be used effectively. Several years ago when various cult groups became active at the University of Delaware, the student-affairs division used a well-organized educational campaign to counter the recruiting efforts of these groups (Sharky, 1984). The public exposure brought to bear from the student newspaper, from educational programs and speakers in the residence halls, and from similar programs in the student union had the effect of alerting the campus population to the activities of these groups. As a result, the groups were unsuccessful in their recruiting efforts and left to seek more fertile grounds for recruiting. The University of Toronto took a similar approach and has held several "Cult Awareness Weeks" to educate its students about cult groups (Max, Han, & Springer, 1985).

Educational programming about cults should be a regular part of the campus program for students but, more importantly, it should be a regular part of the training of new staff--particularly student staff. Student staff who work as resident assistants, orientation leaders, or peer counselors have the closest contact with other students. These students have generally been selected for these positions because of their good human-relations skills and because they offer viable role models for other students. Student staff should be trained to look for some of the warning signs common to people being drawn into cults. The Citizens Freedom Foundation (1983) (now known as the Cult Awareness Network) lists these as: (1) a sudden change in behavior, (2) a breakdown in communication with old friends and increased secretiveness, (3) a sudden rush of new friends who are often off-campus and often "strange", (4) increased talk about how society is evil, (5) change in personality following a retreat with a group and talk about a "conversion experience", and (6) the inability to engage in intellectual discussion without parroting the scripture or dogma of some organization.

Armed with information about recruiting tactics, what to look for in susceptible students, knowledge of campus groups, and common sense, student staff can be one of the most effective sources of information about cult activities on campus. Educating these students is the cornerstone of any well-conceived educational program about cults.

Management of Cult Groups on Campus

Despite educational programs, trained staff, and reasonable standards for recognition of campus organizations, tenacious cult groups will continue to be involved with universities. The question then becomes one of managing their involvement to minimize the associated problems they create for students. One approach was noted above. This is to establish a free-speech area in which cult leaders can be heard and their beliefs and practices openly challenged and debated by the educational community. Another useful approach is to insist that the leaders of the religious cult participate with leaders of the other religious groups on campus in an organization of associated campus ministers, which exists on many campuses. This regular involvement opens avenues of communication among the different denominations, and it can have both an informative and moderating effect on cult leaders.

Regular meetings with cult leaders on campus to express the institution's concern about individual students or the activities of the group are, of course, in order. The closer the contact institutions maintain with cult leaders, the greater the likelihood that the institution may be influential in preventing and resolving student problems.

Conclusion

It is difficult to work with college students and not delight in their success and share their joy as they accomplish some of their major life goals in college. Similarly, it is disturbing to see these same young people become the unwitting victims of unprincipled, self-serving cults. It is hard to ignore these groups as they lay siege to the campus. Administrative apathy and ignorance are their friends. They count on the uninformed administrator to allow them the opportunity to prey upon students.

Colleges and universities have a duty to provide students with an environment which fosters freedom of thought and the development of an educated and principled person. Cults with their coercive and unprincipled tactics rob students of the very things colleges and universities have been organized to teach.

To those who claim that this level of care by university administrators is *in loco parentis*, the answer is "it is." It is the same *in loco parentis* care we extend to students when we impose fire and other safety regulations which threaten their well-being on campus.

Operating within the guidelines of the courts, college administrators should educate students and staff about the practices of cult groups, develop appropriate policies for the recognition of all campus groups, and write policies that address the specific cult behaviors which put our students at risk.

References

Aman v. Handler. (1981). 653 F.2d 41 (lst Cir.).

Anderson, W. (1981). 200 sects reportedly recruit students at Berkeley campus. *The Collegiate Advisor*, August-September, p. 9. (Reprinted from *Pioneer Press*, 1981, May 28).

Biemiller, L. (1983, April 6). Campuses trying to control religious cults. *The Chronicle of Higher Education*, pp. 1, 6-8.

Blimling, G. (1981). Cults, college students, and campus policies. *NASPA Journal, 19*(2), 2-12.

Blimling, G. (1987). Policy issues and administrative considerations in working with extremist religious groups on college and university campuses. In R. Schecter & W. Noyes (Eds.), *Cults on campus: Commentaries and guidelines for college and university administrators*. Framingham, MA: American Family Foundation.

Boyer, G. (1987). *College: The undergraduate experience in America*. New York: Harper & Row.

Bromley, D., & Shupe, A. (1979). *Moonies in America: Cult, church and crusade*, Beverly Hills: Sage Publications.

Burks, S. (1986, April 22). Satan bible feud linked to slaying. *Albuquerque Journal*.

Chapman v. Thomas. (1982). ...F.Sup. ..., No. 80-757-CIV-5, (U.S. Dist. Ct., E.D., NC, Raleigh Div.).

Chess v. Widmar. (1979). 480 F.Supp. 907.

Chess v. Widmar. (1980). 635 F.2d 1310 (App. Ct. 8th Cir.).

Chickering, A. (1972). *Education and identity*. San Francisco: Jossey-Bass.

Citizens Freedom Foundation. (1983). Symptom of cult involvement. Pamphlet.

Clark, J. (1976, August 18 & September 22). Testimony before the *Vermont*

Senate committee for the investigation of alleged deceptive, fraudulent and criminal practices of various organizations in the state.

Clark, J. (1979). Cults. *Journal of the American Medical Association, 243*(3), 179-281.

The Collegiate Advisor. (1983). Maranatha 'deregistration' recommended. *The Collegiate Advisor,* August/September, 7.

Conway,F., & Siegelman, J. (1978). *Snapping: America's epidemic of sudden personality change.* Philadelphia: J.B. Lippincott.

Coons, F. (1974). The developmental tasks of the college student. In D. DeCoster & P. Mable (Eds.), *Student development and education in college residence halls.* Washington, DC: American College Personnel Association.

Cox, H.(1977). Eastern cults and western culture: Why young Americans are buying oriental religions. *Psychology Today, 11*(2), 36-41.

Delgado, R. (1977). Religious totalism: Gentle and ungentle persuasion under the first amendment. *Southern California Law Review,* 51(1), 1-98.

Delgado, R. (1979, February 5). Testimony before a special U.S. Senate Committee entitled *Information meeting on the cult phenomenon in the United States,* (Transcripts of Proceedings).

Douglasv. City of Jeannette. (1943). 319 U.S. 141.

Enroth,R. (1977). *Youth, brainwashing, and the extremist cults.* Grand Rapids, MI: Zondervan.

Erikson, E.H. (1968). *Identity: Youth and crisis.* New York: Norton.

Freshmen characteristics and attitudes. (1984, February 4). *The Chronicle of Higher Education,* pp. 13-14.

Freshmen characteristics and attitudes. (1985, January 16). *The Chronicle of Higher Education,* pp. 15-16.

Galanter, M., Rabkin, R., Rabkin, J., & Deutsch, A. (1979). The "Moonies": A psychological study of conversation and membership in a contemporary religious sect. *American Journal of Psychiatry, 136*(2), 165-170.

Glover v. Cole. (1985) 762 F.2d1197 (App. Ct. 4th Cir.).

Green, M. (1986). A boy's love of Satan ends in murder, a death sentence -- and grisly memories. *People Magazine,* pp. 155-161.

Hassan,S. (1981). Moon organizations. *Ex-Moon Newsletters* (1712 Eye Street, N.W. Suite 1010, Washington, DC 20006).

Havighurst, R.J. (1953). *Human development and education.* New York: Longman's.

Healy v. James. (1972). 408 U.S. 1.

Healy v. James. (1972). 92 S.Ct. 2338.

International Society for Krishna Consciousness v. Barber. (1980). 506

F.Supp. 147 (N.D., New York).

ICEP (September, 1988). Developing an ethical code for proselytizers. *Young People and Cults* (The newsletter of the International Cult Education Program, New York, NY), pp. 2,3, & 6.

Kahn, A.P. (1986). PTA president urges teen cult education. *Cult Observer, 3*(3),2,12. (Reprinted from *PTA Today* (1986, March)).

Kegan v. Delaware. (1975). 349 A.2d 14 (Del.).

Kohlberg, L. (1981). *The philosophy of moral development: Volume one.* San Francisco: Harper & Row.

Langone, M.D., Blood, L. (1990). *Satanism and Occult-Related Violence: What You Should Know.* American Family Foundation.

Lemon v. Kurtzman. (1970). 403 U.S. 602.

Levine, A. (1980). *When dreams and heroes died: A portrait of today's college student.* San Francisco: Jossey-Bass.

Levinson, D.J. (1978). *The seasons of a man's life.* New York: Alfred A. Knopf.

Lynn, B. (1979, February 5). Testimony before a special U.S. Senate Committee entitled *Information meeting on the cult phenomenon in the United States.*

Man charged in stalker murder. (1985, October 25). *USA Today,* p.42.

Max, J., Han, V., & Springer, J. (1985). Cult awareness week at University of Toronto. *The Cult Observer,* November, 11-12. (Reprinted from *The Newspaper,* University of Toronto, 1985, September 18).

People v. Woody. (1964). 61 Cal.2d 716, 394 P.2d 813.

Perry, W., Jr. (1970). *Forms of intellectual and ethical development in the college years.* New York: Holt, Rinehart, & Winston.

Sanford, N. (1967). *Where colleges fail.* San Francisco: Jossey-Bass.

Satan worship rituals on increase. (1984, June). Battle Cry Publications.

Shapiro, E. (1979). Destructive cultism. *American Family Physician,* 15(2), 80-83.

Sharky, S. (1984, March). *Educational programming about cults.* Presented at the annual meeting of the National Association of College Student Personnel Administrators, Louisville, KY.

Singer, M. (1979). Coming out of the cults. *Psychology Today,* 12(8), 72-82.

Solid Rock Foundation v. The Ohio State University. (1979) 478 F.Supp 96 (S.D. Ohio, E.D.).

Stoehr, R. (1978). Why young people join cults. *Campus Ministry Communications.*

Stone, D. (1986, January 3). Satan cult site found. *The Montgomery Journal.*

Tilton v. Richardson. (1971), 403 U.S. 672.

Toffler, A. (1971). *Future Shock.* New York: Bantom Books.

Washington, D. (1986, February 16). Fad or fanatic cult. *El Paso Times.*

Widmar v. Vincent. (1981). 454 U.S. 263.

Wood, J. (1979, February 5). Testimony before a special U.S. Senate Committee entitled *Information meeting on the cult phenomenon in the United States*, (Transcript of Proceedings).

Zorn, E. (1986, April 27). Satan worship called dangerous, growing. *The Chicago Tribune*.

Developing an Ethical Code for Proselytizers

Marcia R. Rudin, MA

The American Family Foundation is conducting a groundbreaking new program with leading Evangelicals and representatives of other religious groups designed to develop an ethical code for proselytizers. This code will be especially useful on college and university campuses where much religious proselytizing takes place. It will provide a useful guide to those who are concerned about cult recruitment at their schools and will help ensure that campus religious activity falls within publicly agreed-upon ethical guidelines.

Several drafts of the code have been written, and work on the document is continuing. (See the model code below.)

"Those of us who study cults and educate the public about them must always carefully define the differences between cults and mainstream religions," says Dr. Michael D. Langone, Executive Director of the American Family Foundation. "One of the goals of the ethical code development program is to help clarify features which distinguish 'fanatics' and 'phonies' from ethical proselytizers. This will help the public to distinguish ethical proselytizers from cultists, show cultists how they must change in order to enter the ethical mainstream of our pluralistic society, and help mainstream religious groups teach their representatives how to maintain ethical behavior when witnessing to their faiths."

Dr. Langone launched the program after several years of AFF research indicated that cultic relationships and other unethical forms of social influence can arise within any group. "We think of cults in terms of their members' behavior, not the group's theology," Langone explains. "It's a tough question of unethically manipulative relationships. Through our interactions with Evangelicals, we at AFF came to realize that complaints we had received about Evangelical groups often involved individual deviations and were not necessarily representative of the behavior of the groups in question. But these ethical lapses caused many people to equate all Evangelicals with controversial cults, a comparison which, of course, disturbs Evangelicals. So I wanted leading Evangelicals and other religious leaders to join with the AFF in developing an effective and comprehensive ethical code that we can all agree on."

Dr. Harold Bussell, formerly Dean of the Chapel at Gordon College in

Wenham, MA, and now Senior Pastor at the Hamilton Congregational Church in Hamilton, MA, is one of the prominent Evangelicals involved in the ethical code project. "It's extremely important that Evangelicals be involved in producing an ethical proselytizing code," Bussell contends. "Not only will it help protect people from abuses by any group, but clarifying guidelines will protect the religious freedom of everyone because it will allow them to present their religious views without being stereotyped as cults. This has been happening to Evangelicals, and it's in our interest to do what we can to prevent that."

According to Bussell, one of the major differences between cults and mainstream religious groups is that the latter oversee their members' behavior and have disciplinary methods to correct it, whereas cults do not. "An ethical code is an absolute necessity," Bussell says. "If Evangelicals had operated by such a code twenty years ago we wouldn't have the problems with disreputable televangelists and aberrant groups that we have today."

Rabbi A. James Rudin, National Director of Interreligous Affairs of the American Jewish Committee, has also participated in the program since its inception. "Historically Jews have always been targeted for aggressive conversionary activity," he says. "While we recognize that it is an important part of the Christian theological agenda, we deeply resent such activity. Having a good ethical code will help ensure that such witnessing will be honest, ethical, and totally aboveboard."

Rudin claims that having even a preliminary draft of the code at his fingertips helps him in his work with Christian groups. "I participated in a heated symposium with some Hebrew Christians several years ago that was sponsored by *Christianity Today* magazine," Rudin explains. "I read the draft ethical code document aloud to them and pointed out how their deceptive recruiting methods go against it. That had a great impact on everyone there."

Rev. Robert Watts Thornburg, Dean of Boston University's Marsh Chapel and Chaplain of the University, cites Rabbi Rudin's experience when he asserts that the ethical code will be most helpful as a pragmatic tool. "The code is to be a model--it's not to be written in stone," Thornburg explains, "and it's not yet clear how it can be enforced. We hope that people will adhere to it through peer pressure and moral persuasion, rather than through legal or official organizational means."

"The people I've talked with are very enthusiastic about the project and want to help formulate a code," Thornburg continues. "In Boston, for several years, we've had encounters with The Boston Church of Christ, a destructive group. In one year over 250 Boston-area college students left school to work for that organization and to recruit other students into it. That experience has sensitized chaplains and college administrators in Boston to the need for a behavior-oriented ethical code that provides guidelines for determining which behaviors are acceptable and which are unacceptable in proselytizing and evangelizing."

Dr. Langone initiated the program 1985, when he asked Reverend Dietrich Gruen, then the Evangelism Specialist and Research Assistant for the Inter-Varsity Christian Fellowship, to assemble a committee of leading Evangelicals to draft an ethical proselytizing code. Gruen's poll of more than one hundred Evangelicals around the country found that approximately two-thirds of them supported the idea of a code. Under Gruen's direction, a team of twelve composed a first draft of an ethical code, basing it on the premise of Article Thirteen of the 1948 United Nations Declaration of Human Rights, which states that "everyone shall have the right to freedom of thought, conscience, and religion," and on the Roman Catholic Church's Second Vatican Council's Declaration on Religious Freedom.

Reverend Gruen and the Inter-Varsity team also contributed to a special issue of *Cultic Studies Journal*, a semiannual interdisciplinary journal published by AFF and edited by Dr. Langone, entitled "Cults, Evangelicals, and the Ethics of Social Influence." The draft code appeared in the journal, which was published in 1985, along with essays contributed by leading Evangelical scholars and others. That special issue of *Cultic Studies Journal* explored questions about such issues as the proper place of proselytizing in an open, pluralistic society, the ethical boundries of proselytizing, and the kinds of accountability mechanisms that should exist in order to help proselytizing groups ensure ethical behavior among their members and the members of other groups participating in our pluralistic society; i.e., what stated codes of ethics, monitoring and training systems, or corrective procedures should there be? The publication generated widespread interest in the project.

In October 1987, Dr. Langone met with distinguished religious leaders including Dr. Bussell, Rabbi Rudin, Rev. Thornburg; Rev. James E. McGuire, STD, Director of the Newman Center at the University of Pennsylvania; Professor Marvin Wilson, Chair of the Department of Biblical and Theological Studies at Gordon College; Dr. Ronald Enroth, sociology professor at Westmont College in Santa Barbara, CA; Rev. James J. LeBar,

Consultant on Cults to the Archdiocese of New York; Reverend Doug Whallon, regional Director for New England of the Inter-Varsity Christian Fellowship; and Jeff Woodward, Area Director for Connecticut of the Inter-Varsity Christian Fellowship. Revs. Thornburg, McGuire, and Whallon assembled and chaired three independent study groups to examine, clarify, revise, and provide a college/university context for the first draft of the ethical proselytizing code devised by Gruen's team.

In the spring of 1988, Reverend Thornburg convened a committee at Boston University to change the draft code into a model, and in June obtained an endorsement of the one-year trial model from the university's Christian Chaplain's Office. On July 15th he met with college chaplains from Harvard, M.I.T., and Boston College to describe the project and obtain their endorsement of Boston University's model code.

"I'm excited by the positive results of these meetings," Rev. Thornburg says. "It's not only a negative--trying to stop abuses and unethical proselytizing--but there's a good spirit from the meetings too. Everyone is involved in this program--Catholics, Jews, Evangelicals, mainline Protestants. It's a genuine breakthrough in interreligous dialogue."

In November, 1990, Rev. Thornburg presented the Ethical Code to a group of Directors of Campus Religious Life from the Division of Higher Education in Boston. "These are coordinators of religious life for students in state and private colleges, including Christian clergy and rabbis," Thornburg explains. "They seemed very interested in the project. I told them the *process* of arriving at an ethical code is more important than the project. I'm trying to keep the issue alive, telling people where we are at the moment."

According to Langone, the long term goals of the ethical code project are the following: 1) to seek additional input from religious groups as well as from communications and cult experts for the further development and refinement of the ethical code; 2) to develop, test, and refine training materials associated with the ethical code; 3) to gain endorsement of the code from authorities across the American religious spectrum; and 4) to establish an interreligous council to provide a non-legal, non-governmental court of appeals in matters of unethical religious influence.

Following is the latest working draft of the Ethical Code:

Revision of a Code of Ethics for Christian Evangelists
as reviewed by

the Ethical Code Study Group on May 24, 1988
(given final approval by Boston University Christian Chaplains
on June 21, 1988)

As Christians engaged in ministry to the campus, we seek to support others who are so engaged. We subscribe to this code of ethical behavior in the hope that we may work in cooperation and mutual support. We accept the obligation to admonish anyone who represents the Christian faith in any manner incompatible with these ethical guidelines or who violates legal requirements set forth by federal or state law, or the regulations of the University.

1. As Christians called by the Living God, we seek to respond to that mandate appropriately in our private and public lives, including our efforts to communicate the Good News about Jesus Christ.

2. As Christians, we seek to follow the mandate, motives, message and model of God in Jesus Christ who invites us to adopt them as our own.

3. We believe all people are created in God's image and therefore we disavow any efforts to influence people which depersonalize or deprive them of their inherent values as persons.

4. Respecting the value of persons, we believe that all persons are worthy of hearing the gospel of Christ. We equally affirm the right of every person to retain his/her own belief options and to make their own decision.

5. We believe in the gospel of Jesus Christ, and affirm the role and goal of the Christian evangelist. However, we do not believe that this justifies any means to fulfill those goals. Hence, we disavow those coercive techniques or manipulative appeals intended to bypass one's critical faculties, play on one's psychological weaknesses, undermine one's relationship with family or religious institutions, or mask the true nature of Christian conversion.

6. While seeking to respect individual integrity, intellectual honesty, and academic freedom of other believers and skeptics, we seek to proclaim Christ/the gospel/faith openly. We reveal our own identity and purpose, out theological positions, and will not be intentionally misleading.

7. As Christian evangelists, we seek to embrace people of other religious persuasions in true dialogue. That is, we acknowledge our common humanity in order to understand, and thus divest ourselves of any stereotypes which are barriers to true dialogue.

Cults on Campus: Training Staff and Educating Students

Training Residence-Hall Staff

Rev. Robert Watts Thornburg

Destructive religious cults prosper and grow in many cases because students feel lonely, isolated, and/or alienated from the campus and society. For example, three cult members find a first-year student sitting alone at breakfast in a large residence hall. They move in with the broad but plastic smiles of so-called "love bombing." Or during final examinations, a cult group begins a new program. Everyone who does programming on campus knows that that time is not a good one to begin a new program, but the cult group looks for a student who has just flunked a crucial exam or who has had a fight with a girlfriend or boyfriend, and they find a prime target.

Cults are disastrously well-suited to basic college conditions: these include the questioning of values and old allegiances and the emergence of bright hopes for the future coupled with an idealism for what may be accomplished. If the college community is to respond effectively, it must respond with the best personnel available, train them satisfactorily, and maintain backup people for support when real trouble is found.

Key Role of the Residence Staff

When a campus is large enough that the Dean of Students or chaplain cannot call every student by his or her first name and know something about the student's personal situation, then the front-line troops become the resident or hall advisors (RA's), student personnel staff who have daily contact with students in their places of residence. As a university chaplain, I believe these student personnel are the most important resources for a well-rounded academic and personal experience in college. They are also among the least rewarded in either financial or emotional support. It is my opinion that the RA's are the ones who can most effectively deal with the destructive cult activities on campus. This can only be accomplished, however, if they are adequately trained, supervised, and supported. This is the way my campus (Boston University) has proceeded.

Preconditions for Effective Programming

There are three basic assumptions underlying this article:

1. Training is valuable either when cults are present on campus or when a potential exists for their presence. If cults are not yet a present danger,

a posture of seeking information, patiently waiting, and cautious observation on the part of senior administration is much wiser than beginning a full-fledged program for a situation which does not yet exist. Be prepared and wait, but do not implement a program too soon, or you will burn out the staff on the issue.

2.   An effective training program must also have the understanding and support of the university administration--for both the trainer and the training program. This is a very volatile issue, and the university administration must be clearly aware of the nature of the problem in order to avoid disastrous consequences.

3.   The trainer must be competently informed about the situation. This understanding must go in two directions: a) The trainer must know the level of involvement, purposes, and procedures of all the major cults that are represented on the campus. While cult behavior is fairly standard from group to group, the training enterprise is much more effective if the trainer knows the historical roots and the basic doctrines of the cults in question. This will require considerable study or the use of previously-trained personnel from outside agencies. b) In addition, it is crucial that the trainer discover the local adaptations made by these groups. In order to adequately train RA's, the trainer must be adequately prepared.

Basic Training Approach

A training event for RA's about destructive cults must be planned jointly by the trainer and the student-personnel staff. (If the Dean of Students and those heading the residence-life program do not perceive that the problem is real, the trainer will be in a very precarious position.)

On large campuses, it is important that the training event take place in small groups rather than in one large group. A group of thirty to forty is about the maximum for adequate training. The trainer is dealing with religious/political/social/psychological issues, and if one is unable to genuinely establish rapport, many serious misunderstandings can develop.

It is also important to be able to hear the very real questions being asked by the RA's. An essential problem arises when cults use language and nomenclature (particularly semi-technical, theological words) which are unfamiliar to many RA's. Therefore, the training event must relieve the nervousness which comes from asking what may be perceived as naive questions. Because the issue is so emotionally charged, the ease and freedom with which the trainer and others talk about religious life and the cults' misuse of religious values makes the training more valuable.

Vital in the presentation is a very basic distinction between belief and behavior. The Constitution of the United States, the charters of many universities, and recent Supreme Court decisions have indicated that we may not use differences in beliefs to exclude a group simply because we disagree with their beliefs or find them distasteful. Unless we can describe behavior which is destructive to the basic purpose of the university, there is no legitimate way to deal with the basic beliefs of cults. The only exception would be on a campus that has doctrinal standards or guidelines for admission.

Informational Presentations

Informational presentations should include at least the following basic questions:

1. "How long have cults been around?" This would include a short historical review of the rise of cults on campus as a phenomenon of the 70's, 80's, and '90's. This is important to consider in order to legitimize the problem, so that students do not become confused with questions about why they have not heard of the difficulties surrounding religious cults before.

2. "What's the problem with the cults anyhow?" It is very important for every trainer to clarify most specifically and articulately this question. I find that cults cut across the essential purpose of the university, which is to be a place for free inquiry and the critique of ideas. Cults tend to foster a simplistic, reductionist solution to the often difficult and complex issues surrounding our daily existence. Cults curtail the free exchange and critical analysis of other religious ideas and notions. In addition, cults tend to take students away from their essential vocational and motivational path, redirecting the student to the purposes and aims of the cult group. Finally, cults exist for their own sake and not for the high and lofty purposes which they proclaim.

3. "How do cults operate?" At this point, it is important that a trainer be able to provide illustrations as specific as possible from the local campus setting so that those being trained can begin to recognize the symptoms of cult involvement. The description of the cult's activities

should progress from the beginning stages of the "love bombing" through the process of disseminating simple ideas which cut one away from other sources of information and friends and tie one more closely to a charismatic leader, to the movement of a person away from the friends he or she has made while participating in the social and academic life of the campus.

4. "What should RA's look for?" The first and most important thing to look for is the "drop out" mentality. A student begins to associate exclusively with a particular new group of friends, and begins to dissociate from older friends and acquaintances. The RA is practically the only person who can recognize this change. Very often, the clue will come from a roommate who is concerned about special tape recordings being played or late-night phone calls. In the more advanced stages, one notices that the student involved in the cult begins to have a significant fall-off in grades and increased participation in late night so-called Bible studies or "soul talks." One other revealing phenomenon we have seen is cult graffiti. In the Bible-based cult groups, these are often standard Christian phrases written on the walls of residence halls.

5. "Does the university have an official policy that can be followed?" This, of course, will depend on the individual philosophy of the university and the extent to which it may clarify its approach to campus organizations in light of the cult phenomenon.

There are some behaviors which are not acceptable, and these need to be adequately addressed. At Boston University there is a clause in the student handbook which prohibits solicitation in residence halls, not only for money, but also for ideological support and votes. This is an effective deterrent to much initial cult solicitation. As a general rule of thumb, invasion of either the living space or the eating space of a student by one who wishes to solicit for a cause of any sort should be considered unacceptable behavior. In the public areas of the university or community, the First Amendment protects the cults' rights to solicit, but in those places a student can freely choose to walk away. When one is confronted while eating, studying, or preparing for bed, then the situation has become very intrusive. In addition, late night phone calls and messages slipped under the door constitute a form of harassment. An RA, when informed of such behavior, can make it clear that such behavior is unacceptable. Requests for moving members of a group into a cluster of rooms in one section of a residence hall may occasionally arise. While schools have differing policies on this matter, students in a cult group who cluster in one section of a residence hall tend to place intense pressure on others in that space who are not in the group.

Traps to be Avoided at all Costs

1. Avoid attacking the beliefs of the cult group. Sometimes it is easy and popular, even humorous, to joke about a cult's religious beliefs, or to attack and belittle these beliefs, as some students may do. This is entirely unacceptable. While trainers should use specific illustrations speaking about the cult doctrines which may adversely affect student life, to belittle such doctrines is very counterproductive and results in greater support being generated among those who demand fair play.

2. Avoid treating all cult groups as if they were alike (e.g. "They all look the same to me.") They are not alike, and failure to appreciate the differences will, in practice, hinder both effective analysis of the situation and counseling.

3. Resist the temptation to exaggerate or confirm false stereotypes. Occasionally, a student will ask whether cults use drugs or sex to attract or maintain members. By and large, cults do not use drugs or sex for these purposes, but even a slight nod of suspicion, not to say a knowing glance, may be seen as confirmation of the charge, however unintentional this result. Such a false impression could destroy the trainer's credibility.

4   Don't create cult martyrs. Cult members will sometimes be at your training sessions. Unless you are straightforward, direct, and honest in your approach, you may make martyrs out of such people and other cult members, who can easily show how unfairly the group is being treated. The educational result, then, may the opposite of your wish because many cult groups suggest to their members that the fate of any true believer will be martyrdom; an attack that seems unfounded or unfair will produce martyrs, make other followers even more devoted, and tend to disarm valid criticism from the wider university community.

5. Finally, training about cults must address the issue of ambiguity, which has two aspects. First, there is a certain ambiguity felt about cults because of the typical contradiction between their high ideals and their corrupt practices and goals. These contradictions must be made clear. Second, it must be understood that the very ambiguity of modern life--felt perhaps most acutely by students who seek clear answers and

guides where there may be none--provides much of the appeal of contemporary cults. As campus leaders, we must not be afraid to decry the cult's simplistic reductionism.

Backup and Support

Dealing with destructive religious cults is not easy for new RA's. The very best training session will only begin the process of alerting them to the dangers which may be involved. The initial session must be followed up with other opportunities for discussion and observation. Without reinforcement, the multitude of responsibilities that RA's have between studies and the requirements of the residence hall tend to make them blind to even the most blatant danger signs. At best, the training will help the RA raise questions but it will not provide any final solutions. There must be further backup.

The well-prepared trainer should have a network of resources, including chaplains and other religious leaders, psychologists, social workers, and others from the campus and the community. The American Family Foundation, which conducts research and provides educational materials in the area of cultism, can be an important resource for both information about the problem and advice on staff training.

Finally, it is important for the trainer to be supportive of an RA who finds a problem, but is unable to deal with it. The more training sessions I do, the more often I have RA's bringing a student with them to have a conversation with me regarding the cult issue. Parents whose children have become involved in cults may make the RA or hall director the first target of their distress, and they will vent considerable wrath on these staff members. Therefore RA's and hall directors must be able to find support from more knowledgeable senior staff in dealing with such situations.

Conclusion

The university campus exists to assist students in the process of reflection and decision-making about the major issues and values of life, to provide pre-professional and professional training for vocational goals, and to clarify the process of analysis and the articulation of ideas.

Religious cults cut across these major purposes. In preparing people to oppose such cults, it is vital that we do not produce a new set of zealots who in their fear of the very real dangers of cults tend to use some of the very procedures or attitudes that are the very ones which we decry. In my several years of planning training sessions with RA's and other residence life staff, I have found that RA's are a vital link in any adequate addressing of the emergence of cults on campus.

Why Resident Assistant Training on Cultism?

Dennis Polselli

First, I would like to explain what a Resident Assistant (RA) does. The expression "overworked and underpaid" holds true for an RA more than for any other undergraduate position on campus. (I am indebted to Gregory S. Blimling and Lawrence J. Miltenberger's excellent book, *The Resident Assistant, Working with College Students in Residence Halls*, (c) 1981, for their insights into this subject.)

Some of the many responsibilities of the RA are performing administrative details, helping to provide control, establishing a healthy residence-hall environment, assisting individual student needs, and providing residence-hall government programs. To help RA's fulfill these responsibilities, we provide them with extensive training programs in such areas as peer counseling, behavior problems, conflict resolution, drug and alcohol abuse, sexuality issues, suicide intervention, and time-management and study skills.

It stands to reason, then, given the above training topics, that not to incorporate information on cultism would be irresponsible on our part because there are many groups clamoring for students' attention.

There are many reasons for students to fall prey to some of these groups, however destructive they may turn out to be. We all long to belong to a community. Students not only want to be accepted, they strive to be somebody, and some groups offer instant power and gratification with no means for the student to find out in advance just how destructive the group can be.

At Framingham State College, we provide training in cultism for RA's at least once a year. It is usually our first workshop. We do this because we have seen evidence that cult groups have knowledge of what new students are going through. Like the RA's, recruiters for some of the groups are slightly older students who have "been there" and know how to use the right techniques to make a student feel wanted and to feel like he/she is somebody.

Our training program provides information on the characteristics of cultic groups and their recruitment methods and techniques, which include mind-control, sleep deprivation, splitting off from families and friends, and total domination. We tell RA's signs of cultic involvement to watch for: students' changes in sleeping habits, not attending classes as much, being away from the residence hall floor and from their friends for long periods of time, and inquiries from parents. We use videotapes such as the one provided by the International Cult Education Program, "Cults: Saying *No* Under Pressure." We provide educational handouts. We open the floor for discussion of any experiences that RA's may be having on their floor based on what they may have heard in the lectures and seen in the videotapes.

Wendy Noyes, Vice President of Student Services at Framingham State College and one of the editors of *Cultism on Campus: Commentaries and Guidelines for College and University Administrators,* published jointly in 1987 by the American Family Foundation and the National Association of Student Personnel Administrators (NASPA), did the first RA training in this area. Then we began to utilize the college's Counseling Center. And I began to study the literature about cults based on an experience I had as a target for recruitment by a cult group fascinated by my blindness and taking advantage of my newness to my job and my recovery from earlier traumatic experiences.

Now, in addition to providing training on my own campus, I do a number of workshops at area RA conferences through which we reach a large number of Boston-area college and university RA staff.

As I always point out in my workshops, being a community builder is the most important duty of the RA, for one-to-one counseling shows an individual that you care. Providing programs and drawing upon students for their talents gives the students the chance to demonstrate their skills to their peers and to learn to truly feel important. Working with an isolated student to fit him/her into the community could very well determine whether or not that student joins a group that will take advantage of his/her feelings and state of mind at any given moment.

RA's are the best group to do this training because they spend about eighty percent of their time in residence halls. This is why we put so much emphasis on RA training and spend the money we do on this area of student-affairs programming.

RA's are our links to the students, and we must arm them to the teeth with all we know about groups in our society that may be destructive. Our RA's must be the first line in our defense. We must also make RA's aware of elementary laws that protect the right to freely associate, for in the case of public colleges and universities, banning cultic groups is not always practical. Then we must urge the RA's to present programs on cultism on their floors to further spread the word. For in this case, education is the best and only weapon there is to keep our students freely thinking and challenging and questioning instead of accepting everything in life at face value.

Working With Cult-Affected Families

Michael D. Langone, Ph.D.

During the last two decades, increasing numbers of parents have consulted mental health professionals dealing with a child in a cult. At the American Family Foundation, my colleagues and I have worked with several thousand parents. Two cult clinics run by the Jewish Board of Family and Children's Services in New York and the Jewish Federation of Los Angeles have each worked with more than 1000 families. Since several million people have been affected by cultic groups, thousands of other families have probably consulted mental health professionals not connected with any of these organizations.

Although the mental health community seems to be more responsive to the needs of this population than it was in the past, many mental health professionals are not aware of the following clinical findings:

.   The majority of cult members are psychologically normal, although a sizable minority (30%-50%) appear to have had psychological problems that predate the cult experience (Clark, 1979; Conway & Siegelman, 1982; Galanter, 1989). Given, however, that recent epidemiological data indicate that 20% of the general population is diagnosable (Friedman, 1986), the cult population is probably not markedly different from the norm.

.   Cultic environments, which are highly manipulative and exploitative, can cause psychiatric symptomatology that one would not expect given a person's psychological history. Indeed, Atypical Dissociative Disorder, and even occasionally Post-Traumatic Stress Disorder, have been used to describe cult-related psychopathology.

.   Although some families who seek help with cult-related problems are seriously disturbed and/or use the cult to hide family problems, the majority of families seeking help are normal and are concerned because they detect real and alarming changes in the cult-involved family member (Clark, Langone, Schecter, & Daly, 1981; Maron, 1988; Sirkin & Grellong, 1988).

If mental health professionals consulted by a cultist's family keep these three observations in mind, they will be able to complete the first and most important task in working with this population: to listen to the family's concerns, no matter how strange they may sound.

Four task areas call for ongoing attention: assessment, education, treatment, and training.

Assessment

Assessment of cultists' families should take advantage of as many data sources as possible, in part because the key person in the family, i.e., the cult member, is either unavailable or uncooperative. I utilize interviews, questionnaires (Langone, 1983), letters written to and from the cult member, resource material on the cult in question (including that produced by the cult), and any other pertinent information. I try to get general background information on the cultist, his or her family, and the group. When, where, and how did he or she join the group? What is the group's name? How old is the convert? How many children are in the family? I also evaluate the family's strengths and weaknesses, psychiatric history, conflict areas, and problem-solving style. A unified family is usually much more effective in helping a member harmed by cult involvement. Religious background is sometimes significant, especially when the group is a religious cult. Jewish parents whose child has joined a Christian cult or Christian parents whose child has joined a Hindu cult may, for example, have to deal with feelings of betrayal in addition to other disturbing reactions.

Inquiry into the family's experiences with the group and the cultist's behavior since joining it can illuminate how a particular group has affected a particular person. It is not sufficient to label a group "destructive," because not everyone exposed to the same group will respond in the same way: some may be devastated; others may remain unscathed. Assessing the impact of a cult environment requires, of course, some investigation of the cultist's developmental and psychological history. Pre-cult schizophrenic tendencies, for example, could render a person especially vulnerable to a group characterized by extensive use of hypnotic exercises which blur the boundary between self and other.

A key question which helps focus the assessment and disentangle valid family concern from "cult hysteria" is the following: "If your child were not in a cult, what, if anything, would bother you about his or her behavior?" This question helps the family and therapist identify specific detrimental changes *before* they speculate about what caused the disturbing problems. Although this may seem self-evident, those families (the majority in my experience) who have learned a little about cults and mind control before they seek help tend to let their theory, i.e., "my kid is under mind control," structure their observations, rather than vice versa. I try to begin with the behavior and then make inferences about what caused it. More often than not, mind control is, in fact, a significant factor.

Focusing on behavior, however, helps the family identify other significant factors such as pre-cult psychological problems and identify concrete behavioral changes that they would like to effect (for example, increased frequency of communication between parents and a cult-involved child.) Focusing on concrete behaviors also helps families understand the need to establish a hierarchy of goals such as improving communication skills, increasing frequency of contacts, finding out about what their family member is doing/thinking/feeling, improving rapport, and asking the family member to get "the other side of the story" from exit counselors. My fundamental objective is to help families devise an ethical strategy for helping their family member make an informed reevaluation of his/her cult involvement.

Education

If in fact a family member does appear to have been harmed by a highly manipulative group, it is generally advisable to help family members learn about the psychological processes that constitute mind control, brainwashing, coercive persuasion, thought reform, or whatever terminology one prefers. Association with grass-roots organizations such as the Cult Awareness Network can provide helpful information and support for many families, as well as access to video and audiotapes, ex-members of various cults, and written materials.

Treatment

Training, or consultation, consists of teaching family members about the cult-conversion process and helping them improve their communication skills and devise ethical influence strategies. Frequently, however, families are so disturbed by a member's cult involvement that they need psychological or psychiatric treatment. Sometimes the training process can proceed while treatment is occurring; sometimes the training process and all work aimed at helping the cult member must be put on hold while the family members try to get a handle on the emotional reactions that render them at least partly dysfunctional.

Problem areas that often require direct interventions include severe marital or family conflict, depressive reactions, anxiety reactions, and the exacerbation of long-standing psychological difficulties. Although standard psychotherapeutic techniques can be helpful, successfully resolving or managing these problems requires that the family members learn about the cult-conversion process. Their emotional reactions usually result from confusion, fear, and despair elicited by unsuccessful attempts to persuade the cult-involved family member to leave a destructive situation. The family members must come to understand enough about the cult-conversion process to regain hope and patience or else the ongoing frustration of standing by helplessly while a loved one is in danger will continually fuel the emotional reactions against which traditional therapeutic techniques are directed.

Occasionally, however, the family's situation is indeed hopeless, and their only viable course is to grieve the loss of the cult-involved family member and go on with their lives. Doing this is extremely difficult, especially for parents of a cult-involved child. Because the child is alive, a shred of hope always remains, no matter how high the level of despair. One mother, for example, described her situation as "being at my child's wake, but there's no body."

Training

Deciding to teach a family skills for helping a cult-involved member presumes at least one of the following: a) the family member probably is in an environment that is destructive to him or her, b) the family wants to help the member make a voluntary reevaluation, c) with assistance, the family can probably succeed in this goal, or d) the family has so little information, but enough reason for concern, that they need assistance in devising a strategy to collect enough information to determine whether or not to intervene.

Once the decision to proceed is made, training, or consultation, should address the following issues:

. Collecting Information: Most people are more concerned with articulating their point of view than testing it. Since cult-related situations involve much uncertainty and ambiguity, it is important that family members not become complacent opinion-givers. They should be taught how to be "practical scientists," encouraged to treat their observations and inferences as hypotheses to be tested through the reasonably systematic collection of relevant information.

In addition to the information sources mentioned earlier, families should be encouraged to find out about the group with which their member is involved and, most importantly, to find out what the cult-involved family member thinks, feels, and does. Families must be taught to cut back on giving advice and to pay more attention to asking questions. Otherwise they will not be able to make informed decisions or be as rational as they want the cult-involved person to be.

Establishing Ethics: Families attempting to help a member voluntarily reevaluate a cult involvement face an apparent ethical dilemma. On the one hand, they may condemn the cult for using deceptively manipulative techniques of persuasion and control. On the other hand, they may not be able to avoid at least a mild use of such techniques in order to facilitate a voluntary reevaluation of cult involvement.

This dilemma is more apparent than real because the ethical propriety of techniques of persuasion and control depends upon the magnitude of deception and manipulation, the goals of the interaction, and the context in which it takes place. These three factors differ significantly in cultic and family relationships. The family's goal is to protect and advance their family member's well-being; the cult's goal is to fulfill the leader's wishes. The family's manipulations are mild; the cult's are extreme. The family functions within the context of an open society which encourages autonomy and the free flow of information; the cult is a closed society which fosters dependency and systematically inhibits a free flow of information. Moreover, a person's family traditionally has more ethical latitude in social influence processes involving family members than do outsiders. Hence, if families do not employ extremely unethical means of influence and if they continually pay attention to the ethical dimension of their own behavior, they are not likely to go beyond the bounds of ethical propriety.

Improving Communication: By the time most families seek professional assistance, some estrangement of the cult-involved member has already occurred. Families who respond emotionally or authoritatively usually feed into the cult's attempts to isolate the involved person from significant others. In most cases, therefore, professionals need to teach families basic communication skills, e.g., the difference between "I-statements" and "you-statements," in order to build rapport. Families must realize they cannot have any constructive influence if they have little or no contact with the involved person. And they cannot increase the amount of contact if they do not have the communication skills to maintain or build a rapport.

Modifying the Field of Forces Impinging on the Cult-Involved Member

In working with families, I employ a diagram in which I place the cult-involved person between boxes representing the cult and the mainstream world. The following three forces affect the cultist from both directions: appeal, recoil, and manipulative pull. "Appeal" refers to those aspects of the cult and mainstream world that are genuinely gratifying to the cultist: e.g., friendships and vocational challenges. "Recoil" refers to those aspects of the cult and mainstream world that cause doubt, fear, or discouragement. "Manipulative pull" refers to the mind-control factor, and is, of course, a strong force pulling the person toward the cult. In the case of the cult, however, manipulative processes such as the use of chanting to suppress doubts are used to lower the cultist's awareness of cult-based recoil.

The consultant's task is to help the family modify the field of forces so as to increase the cultist's capacity to make an informed, voluntary reevaluation of his/her cult involvement. Initially, families tend to argue with the cultist about the mind-control factor, the manipulative pull. This is often unproductive--family members tend to get too emotional and, to the extent that they succeed in arousing doubts in the cultist, he/she tends to suppress the doubts or to retreat from the family. Consequently, families should be made aware of the other forces and how they can be modified. They should try to reconnect the cultist to those aspects of the mainstream world that he/she genuinely liked, while simultaneously making him/her aware of how the genuine gratifications of the cult can be obtained in the mainstream world.

Family members' growing understanding of the mind-control process should be used to teach them how to subtly and tactfully increase the cultist's awareness of cult-based recoil. One mother, for example, while visiting her daughter living in squalid conditions in an Eastern-based religious group, feigned an innocent curiosity about a beautiful house on the hill (where the leader lived). In so doing, she succeeded in making her daughter more aware of the discrepancy between the leader's and followers' living conditions without angering or frightening her and precipitating a defensive suppression of thoughts critical of the leader.

The mental-health professional can play a special role in helping families understand the cultist's recoil from the mainstream world. Sometimes this recoil results from unmanaged developmental problems such as vocational confusion. Sometimes it results from deep-rooted psychological problems. When mainstream recoil is strong, cultists may tend to stay in their groups even if they are unhappy, for the solution--leaving and going back to their old problems--is more frightening than the problems engendered by cult affiliation. In these cases, it is important to be aware of the cultist's psychological history in order to offer families advice on how to increase the cultist's confidence that he/she can learn to manage mainstream-based problems.

Post-Cult Adjustment

Many cultists experience considerable difficulty when they leave their groups. Some who have spent years in a group may suffer from "maturational arrest," that is, their psychological development may lag many years behind their chronological age. Others return to old psychological problems that had merely been placed in storage during their time in the cult. Many experience symptoms directly related to the cult experience such as the dissociation ex-cultists call "floating." Psychological reactions include depression, guilt, anger, anxiety, bitterness, and a periodic resurgence of the desire to return to the illusory security of the group.

Mental health professionals can help families deal with these difficulties by making them realize that their problems don't necessarily end when the cultist leaves the group and returns home. Although professionals can help by providing therapy to the former cultist, family members must provide the day-to-day support ex-cultists need as they try to get their lives in order.

References

Anderson, S., & Zimbardo, P. (1984). On resisting social influence. *Cultic Studies Journal, 1* (2), 196-220.

Andres, R., & Lane, J. (Eds.). (1988). *Cults & consequences: The definitive handbook.* Los Angeles: Commission on Cults & Missionaries, Community Relations Committee, Jewish Federation Council of Greater Los Angeles.

Clark, J.G. (1979). Cults. *Journal of the American Medical Association, 242,* 179-181.

Clark, J.G., Langone, M.D., Schecter, R.E., & Daly, R.C.B. (1981). *Destructive cult-conversion: Theory, research, and treatment.* Weston (MA): American Family Foundation.

Conway, F., & Siegelman, J. (June, 1982). Information disease. *Science Digest.*

Friedman, D.X. (1986). Psychiatric epidemiology counts. *Archives of General Psychiatry, 41*, 931-933.

Galanter, M. (1989). *Cults: Faith, healing, and coercion*. New York: Oxford University Press.

Hassan, S. (1988). *Combatting cult mind control*. Rochester (VT): Park Street Press.

Langone, M.D. (1983). Family Cult Questionnaire: Guidelines for professionals. Weston (MA): American Family Foundation.

Lifton, R.J. (1961). *Thought reform and the psychology of totalism*. New York: Norton.

Maron, N. (1988). Family environment as a factor in vulnerability to cult involvements. *Cultic Studies Journal, 5* (1), 23-43.

Ross, J.C., & Langone, M.D. (1989). *Cults: What parents should know*. New York: Carol Publishing Group.

Sirkin, M.I., & Grellong, B. (1988). Cult vs. non-cult Jewish families: Factors influencing conversion. *Cultic Studies Journal, 5* (1), 2-23.

Schein, E. (1961). *Coercive persuasion*. New York: Norton.

Singer, M.T. (1986). Group psychodynamics. *Merck Manual*, fifteenth edition, Psychiatry Section. Rahway (NJ): Merck, Sharp, & Dohme.

West, L.J., & Singer, M.T. (1980). Cults, quacks and the nonprofessional psychotherapies. In H.I. Kaplan, A.M. Freedman, & B.J. Sadock (Eds.), *Comprehensive textbook of psychiatry, III*. Baltimore: Williams and Wilkens.

Counseling Cult-Impacted Students

Lorna Goldberg, ACSW and William Goldberg, ACSW

When a college counselor is approached to help a student with a cultic involvement, effective response will depend upon the stage of cult involvement of the student. The counselor may be approached during the initial recruitment of the cultist, during the active stage of cult involvement, or after the student has decided to leave the group. Since the student is likely to be in a different frame of mind in each of these situations, each requires a different combination of strategies.

Initial Recruitment

First, a counselor may be approached by a student who is uncertain about spending a weekend with a cultic group or who is considering joining such a group. The most important intervention, in this case, is to break the momentum of the organization's recruiting strategy by helping the student to postpone his/her decision. The student's enthusiasm and desire to find an idealistic path should be acknowledged, but the counselor should model an appropriately questioning attitude. Has the student researched the track record of the organization in question or relied on the veracity of the recruiter for this information? Has the student spoken to individuals who are former members to gain their perspective on why they left?

It may be helpful to point out to the student similarities in the recruiting process and the student's experiences in other high-pressure sales situations. The dynamics are the same, except that, in this case, the sales person is trying to sell the customer an idea rather than a product. Remind the student that just as a wise consumer doesn't rely on the salesperson for all information on a product, a wise consumer of ideas shouldn't rely solely on a proselytizer.

Remember that the student would not approach you for guidance on this issue unless he/she felt some discomfort about joining a group. Your role is to help the student bring these healthy cautionary feelings to the surface.

Organizations such as the American Family Foundation, the Cult Awareness Network, and the International Cult Education Program can provide you and the student with valuable information on specific groups. FOCUS, the national organization of former cult members, can also be helpful. Telephone calls to colleagues at other colleges and universities who may have had experience in dealing with this particular group may also be enlightening.

Active Involvement

The student may approach the couselor while in the active stage of cult involvement. Although during this stage the counselor is more likely to be approached by the student's friend, roommate or family than the student him/herself, the student may recognize that something is wrong and seek help from a trusted professional.

In this situation, the counselor must, of course, first deal with the issues the student is presenting. As the counselor gains the student's trust, the cult's tenets which are causing problems for the student can be discussed. The counselor's attitude toward the cult should be respectful but questioning (as opposed to critical) of the basic premises upon which the cult's philosophy is based. For example, the counselor may point out that philosophers and theologians have struggled for centuries over the issues which the cult leader claims to have resolved once and for all. The cult leader is not the first in history to have made these claims, and most of the others have been proven to be false prophets. How does the student know that this individual has THE ANSWER? If the student is following his/her gut feeling, ask if his/her gut feelings have ever been wrong. How will the student know when this group is no longer meeting his/her needs? What will the signs be? If the student learns something that casts a different light on the subject, does he/she have the strength to admit a mistake was made?

The counselor might ask the student if he/she would be willing to speak with someone who has left this organization or who knows more about it and can offer a different perspective. If the student insists upon first checking with the group's leadership, the counselor should say that this is an excellent opportunity because it will help the student see how much integrity and openness the group has. The counselor can point out that any open organization encourages its members to explore ideas and possibilities; only a group with something to hide would tell people they will be harmed by hearing negative things about it. By framing the issue in this manner the counselor helps the student to question the group's motivations if, indeed, he/she has been told not to speak to a so-called "backslider."

The counselor should attempt to keep the lines of communication open with the cultist even if they disagree about an issue. As long as they continue to engage in a dialogue, there is a chance the cultist can be helped. Focus on the group's methods, not its ideology. For example, it is not wise to engage in a discussion of interpretations of scripture when an individual has joined a Bible cult unless the counselor is a Biblical scholar. Instead, the counselor should attempt to focus the dialogue on concrete issues and on observations of the group's methods. The counselor should grant the student permission to be questioning and skeptical about these practices.

When the Student Leaves a Group

The third situation in which the college counselor is likely to be approached for help in a cultic situation is after the student has decided to leave the group and is trying to resume his/her life and education. The most important task at this point is for the student to see him/herself as someone who temporarily deviated from a career or educational path and not see him/herself primarily as a former cultist. Although it is important, of course, for the student to deal with issues stemming from the past cult membership and residual feelings and symptoms (see Singer, "Coming out of the Cults" and Goldberg and Goldberg, "Group Work with Former Cultists") it is also important that the student not define him/herself *solely* as someone who made a terrible mistake by joining a cult.

The counselor can be helpful during this period by assisting the student to put the cult experience into perspective. In most cases, cultists do not consciously decide to join a group. Instead, they are tricked and manipulated into joining. The counselor should help the student see that it is unfair to judge him/herself by facts which were not available when the student joined.

Many former cultists continue to see the cult and the cult leader as powerful and to fear retribution for leaving the cult. It is helpful for the counselor to point out that the cult has only as much power as the former member is willing to relinquish to it. Role-playing potentially tense situations such as meeting a cult member on campus can be a helpful technique at this time.

On the other hand, if the student is interested in speaking out publicly about the cult, this action should be encouraged. It is a healthy way to feel active rather than passive, it reinforces the student's decision to leave, and it performs a public service. In the authors' experience, it is almost always beneficial. Of course, if the student prefers to maintain a low profile, that decision should also be respected.

Finally, the counselor can help former cultists by referring them to the

FOCUS network of ex-members. Peers who have lived through similar experiences can often offer more support, advice, and help than professionals. It is very helpful for former cultists to learn that others have survived the experience and have moved on with their lives.

References

Lorna Goldberg and William Goldberg, "Group Work with Former Cultists," *Social Work,* 27 (March, 1982)

Margaret Singer, "Coming Out of the Cults," *Psychology Today,* 12 (January, 1979)

How Campus Law Enforcement Personnel Can Monitor Cult Activities

Larry Kahaner and Larry Zilliox, Jr.

In the last few years, campus law enforcement administrators have become aware that cult recruiters are active at colleges and universities. Because cult groups often operate secretly and deceptively, campus law enforcement officials will sometimes have to use investigative techniques to gather necessary information about these groups. We will describe here some techniques which may be helpful.

A word of caution: both community and campus law-enforcement officials' concerns about cults and satanic groups should be confined to these groups' *destructive actions*--harming others, law-breaking, or criminal activities--and not their beliefs or ideologies. Although individuals and religious groups have freedom of belief, they don't have freedom to engage in illegal, harmful, or violent acts.

Investigating cults on campus can be a complex process, so we'd like to share some of our methods with you.

Examining Original Source Material

We believe one of the most important sources of information about a campus group, and a source that's often not fully utilized, is material the group itself distributes on your campus. This includes pamphlets, books, video and audiotapes which the group produces to recruit people, sell to members, be used by outsiders, or all of the above.

As you study the media, always remember that they were produced to show what the group wants people to know: in other words, they're propaganda and not necessarily the truth, and should be treated as such. On the other hand, you can learn a great deal by studying these materials closely.

Pamphlets are the most common form of original source material you will encounter on your campus. Notice how the pamphlet is presented. A slick, colorful, expensively-printed brochure says a great deal about a group. It shows they're well-organized, conscious of their appearance to outsiders, and perhaps affluent. Clearly, a corporate-quality brochure shows that a group has done well financially. It may have wealthy backers or many members.

A poorly-assembled brochure or pamphlet may indicate a loosely organized group or one that can't afford a handsome presentation. A photocopied pamphlet may indicate that the group is just getting started, has few members, or is fragmented.

Although this may seem obvious, the pamphlet can tell you the exact name of the group, which may differ from its campus name. For instance, a fictional group we'll call "The Oasis" may really be named "The Oasis of Divine Love and Spirituality, Inc." Note that it may not necessarily be registered in the state in which you received the pamphlet.

Next, notice the address. It will tell you if the group is actually operating on your campus, on a different campus, or nearby. If the address is on a different campus, contact its law enforcement officials to see if they've done any investigating or have had any experience with the group. Because colleges and universities are such fertile recruitment grounds for cults, if a group is operating on your campus they've probably operated on others as well.

On the pamphlet you may also see phone numbers, pictures of the leader, buildings they own and other pertinent information. These can be checked out.

Make a note of any dates on the pamphlet. These may indicate how long the cult has been active.

Check the printing company used. It may be cult-related or simply have been printed by the lowest bidder. This may be an angle worth pursuing.

The pamphlet may mention that the group is tax-exempt and that donations are tax deductible. Make note of it. This bit of information will allow you to request information about the group from the Internal Revenue Service. If the group solicits donations on campus it should also be registered with state agencies.

Even though, as we've mentioned above, a group will tell you in its material only what it wants you to know, pay attention to what it has to say. Very often a group will print all or part of its doctrine or ideology in the brochure.

Everything we've written about pamphlets applies to books also. However, the publishing of a book shows a more organized, better-funded group, which in itself is a significant piece of information. A high-quality video or audiotape product is also a strong indication of a well-organized and well-financed organization because professional-level videotape production is expensive. Note who wrote, directed, and produced the product.

Other Investigative Procedures

Establish special reporting procedures to identify incidents involving campus groups. The information you collect doesn't necessarily have to be negative. Build a file for each active group. If nothing else, it may help you answer questions about the group from concerned parents and administrators.

Be alert to activities or literature attacking other student groups. Some larger cults have been known to monitor other campus groups, especially radical political groups, and send information about their activities to law enforcement officials in an attempt to discredit them.

Cults may target students with access to school computers so they can use them for cult activities.

Cults may also target faculty members and use them to identify possible recruits.

Be aware of student-distributed flyers for local businesses, especially restaurants, which may be cult-owned.

One common type of cult fraud is in the area of student loans. Some cults have members enroll in an institution, obtain a loan, then drop out. They may do this at many schools. (One example is the conviction on this charge recently of the leader of a group in New Jersey known as The Circle of Friends.)

Monitoring Satanic and Other Ritual Activities

College students may join satanic groups in order to gain a sense of belonging or because they want direction during a confusing time in their lives. Satanism attracts many because of its promise of personal power and ego-fulfillment gained through tapping a power higher than themselves.

Also, young people are attracted to satanic groups during their rebellious college years because they know what they're doing is repugnant to their families, friends, school, and community. Engaging in occult activities sets them apart and makes them feel special and unique. Another draw is that satanism may give an ideological justification for engaging in a indulgent lifestyle (Langone and Blood, 1990).

The methods mentioned above for investigating cult groups apply to examining satanic and other occult activities also. But investigating satanic groups is more difficult because most don't make their actions public. They rarely solicit donations or recruit openly on campus.

However, unlike other cults, satanic groups often engage in rituals that leave evidence behind. For example, a group may perform an outdoor ritual and build a brazier or fire pit as part of that activity. In other cases, investigators may find small animals that have been sacrificed, inverted crosses, or graffiti with occult writings.

A word of caution: finding some indication of occult activity, especially graffiti, doesn't necessarily indicate large-scale or regular activity by a satanic group. Perhaps students are just defacing property to disturb the school administration and other students. Often young people may wear certain amulets or other pieces of jewelry because they like the way they look--it's simply fashion and not evidence of occult beliefs.

Keep in mind that students may use the social bonding mechanism, a camaraderie, *esprit de corps*, and underground organization of a satanic group as an excuse to perform illegal and immoral acts. The acts themselves may have little or no relation to religious beliefs (Langone and Blood, 1990).

References

Langone, M.D. and Blood, L.O. (1990). *Satanism and occult-related violence: what you should know*. Weston, MA: American Family Foundation, pp. 44-47.

A Multi-Faceted Approach to
Preventive-Education Programs about Cults

Ronald N. Loomis

Since 1979, I have presented hundreds of cult-awareness programs to thousands of people. I now average about one hundred such programs each year. After more than a decade of experience with a variety of approaches to educating students regarding the harmful effects of destructive cults, I have concluded that the best approach is a multi-faceted one. Conducting a variety of different kinds of programs in a variety of different settings and offering them throughout the academic year has proven to be very effective at reaching a maximum number of students.

Why Present Cult-Awareness Education Programs?

Cults are prevalent throughout contemporary society and are particularly present on college and university campuses. In most cases, the groups claim to be legitimate. Many are even registered as campus organizations. If they are not violating the law or campus regulations, there is no basis for restricting them or banning them from campus. Yet we know that they pose a significant threat to the safety and well-being of students. The only resolution for that dilemma is for the institution to provide programs which educate students about the techniques used by cults to deceive, manipulate, coerce, and exploit them, so that students can recognize and resist them.

It is important to provide this information because there may be cults active on your campus. But even if there aren't, this information will be helpful to your students when they are not on your campus, for example, while they are traveling during breaks or particularly after they graduate. I know many students who were recruited while on a summer job away from home or while making the transition from college after graduation.

Different Settings for Programs

I have had experience with all of the following types of programs and have found each of them to be effective for a particular segment of the student body:

1. Campus-wide lectures, presented by national or regional experts on various aspects of the cult phenomenon, sponsored by campus programming boards.

2.   Smaller, more intimate presentations for students living in a particular residence hall. Sometimes these are done for the residents of a particular wing or floor.

3.   After-dinner presentations in fraternities and sororities, particularly on date night.

4.   Classroom presentations as a guest lecturer for a course. Presentations on cults and mind control are of particular interest to faculty who teach courses in psychology, sociology, journalism, creative writing, etc.

5.   Appearances on campus or local radio and television programs, particularly phone-in talk programs.

6.   In-service training programs for student peer counselors such as resident advisors in residence halls.

7.   Presentations to officers of campus organizations as part of the student activities leadership-development training series.

8.   Presentations to members of campus organizations such as clubs or religious groups.

9.   Providing background information to campus newspapers, enabling them to do feature articles about specific groups which are recruiting on that campus.

10. Presentations to faculty or staff groups.

Different Types of Presentations

There are many different types of presentations which can by used to provide information and to stimulate discussion. Among the ones that I have found to be effective are the following:

1.   Lectures which provide an overview of the cult phenomenon using transparencies or slides to impact the audience visually and graphically as well as orally.

2.   Presentations by former cult members who are willing to describe their own experiences. Hearing from someone like themselves is a

particularly effective way to reach young people.

3   Films or videotapes on various aspects of the cult phenomenon. There are many good ones available, both dramatizations and documentaries. An excellent resource is the videotape produced by the International Cult Education Program (ICEP), "Cults: Saying *No* Under Pressure." It features Charlton Heston as the moderator, several national experts, a dramatization of a cult recruitment scene, former cult members, parents, clergy, and a very entertaining mentalist/magician.

Suggested Content of Presentations

While there are many different approaches to cult-awareness presentations, I suggest the following as a basic outline of essential information to be included. (If you wish to receive a more complete outline of my program, contact the International Cult Education Program.)

Part I - Overview of Cult Phenomenon

1.   What is a Cult?

    A. Dictionary Definitions
    B. Historical Evolution of Cults
    C. Characteristics of Cults
    D. Scope of the Cult Problem in Contemporary Society
    E. Scope of the Cult Problem on College Campuses

2.   Six Types of Groups

    A. Religious
    B. Therapy
    C. Political
    D. Commercial
    E. New Age
    F. Satanic/Ritualistic Abuse

3.   Characteristics of Cults

    A. Deception
    B. Use of Mind Control or "Brainwashing" in Indoctrination
    C. Exploitation
    D. Psychological Entrapment

Are These Programs Effective?

For the first few years, I had no idea if the programs were really effective. But after more than a decade of presentations I now get calls from students or recent graduates who tell me that they recently had an encounter with a cult recruiter and that even when the approach was deceptive they remembered some things they had learned from my presentation a few years earlier and recognized what was really happening to them. Armed with that awareness, they were able to terminate the recruitment episode. If by informing students about the techniques used by these groups to deceive and exploit them we can prevent *one student* from being recruited into a cult, then our efforts will have been worthwhile.

University of California - Berkeley's Cult-Awareness Efforts

Marcia R. Rudin, MA

Concerned about the increase in cult activity on the University of California - Berkeley campus and about the number of students affected by cults, the Student Activities and Services Department there instigated an intensive cult awareness program for students, faculty, and staff in the autumn of 1989.

Hal Reynolds, a student affairs officer in the Office of Student Activities and Services at Berkeley, is spearheading the effort. According to Reynolds, cult groups set up tables on the campus at Sproul Plaza, organize rallies, schedule recruiters to cover the Plaza, hold meetings and lectures, and recruit in residence halls and other campus locations.

In June of 1989 Reynolds organized an Ad-Hoc Campus Cult Awareness Network, a group of approximately twenty Berkeley staff, counselors, student advisors, attorneys, and professors. Its cult-education efforts include the following:

1. Revising and reprinting a flyer for students, prepared by the office of Religious Affairs, which highlights characteristics of cult groups and outlines steps for seeking help;

2. Preparing a statement of procedural guidelines for campus staff;

3. Preparing an informational reference brochure for campus staff;

4. Providing training programs for residence counselors and orientation-program interns;

5. Establishing a campus cult-awareness center and network;

6. Developing cult counseling skills for campus counselors;

7. Providing information on cults to local media.

The Berkeley campus cult-awareness center and network has developed four major projects. These include providing an information session about cults during Berkeley's orientation week, setting up a table on the Sproul Plaza Walkway on Activities Day so interested students can sign up to be a part of a student resource network, establishing an organization for students to share past cult experiences, and preparation of resource materials.

According to Reynolds, the student resource network, called SCAT (Student Cult Awareness Team), "has been the most interesting project and has been very useful to other Berkeley students." SCAT is composed of eight to ten students, several of whom have done extensive research into various cult groups. "Some of these students have helped their friends who are in cults," Reynolds says. "And SCAT provides a support group for other students who have friends in cults."

When You're Asked about Cults

Robert C. Fellows, MTS

Probably the two questions that I am asked most often about cults are "How can you tell if a group is a cult?" and "What can I do if I know someone who is in a cult?"

Identifying a Destructive Group

In asking the first question, people usually mean, "How can I tell if a group is destructive?" A group can be deviant or heretical without being destructive. A group can also be destructive without holding particularly unusual beliefs.

Dr. Michael D. Langone of the American Family Foundation defines a destructive group as one that is manipulative and deceptive, exclusive, psychologically or financially exploitative, totalitarian, and/or psychologically damaging to its members or their families.

A group can be destructive without claiming to be a new religion or self-improvement method. Rather than attempting to determine if a group is a "cult," I try to get people to see how any group, and even a personal relationship, can be destructive to individual freedom if it is manipulative.

Some Characteristics of Destructive Groups

.   Exclusive: The group claims or implies that they have the only right answer to a specific question or problem.

.   Totalitarian: The members are always expected to think, feel, and act in a manner prescribed by the group.

.   Psychologically damaging to the cult member or to his/her family: This is seen especially with groups that try to separate members from their families.

Counseling the Cult Member

You can help someone who has undergone a sudden personality change or who is a member of a destructive group.

The techniques for communicating with those who are involved in manipulative groups consist primarily of active listening and creating an environment for change.

Keep lines of communication open. If you are the member's friend or part of the family, leave the door open for him/her to come back at all times. Use active listening and remain calm. Make sure they know that you hear them. Make "I" statement about your position and feelings, and don't humor them. At the same time, avoid ultimatums, orders, force, punishment, or rewards for leaving the group. Don't try to buy his/her mind.

Communication with family and friends is most important for reintegration into life away from the group. Talk about the member's past, former relationships, and life before the radical change. Maintain communication with others in the member's life as you counsel him/her.

Keep arguments about the beliefs of the group to an absolute minimum. This is especially difficult to do. Avoid polarization, name-calling, and the misuse of the word "cult." Remember: deviant or heretical views by your standards are not necessarily destructive. Try not to deny other desires for spiritual meaning. Remain open minded and avoid rigid positions. Focus on the restriction of free choice due to manipulation and deception.

Learn as much as you can about the group so that you can discuss it intelligently with the member. To learn about its beliefs, you can read the group's own literature. To learn about the group's activities, contact the American Family Foundation or the Cult Awareness Network. Both have collections of published articles about specific groups they can send you.

Choose a therapist who is a specialist in exit counseling. Avoid therapists who use coercive deprogramming or who employ psychologically dangerous models of therapy. Make sure that any lawyers you retain are specialists in cult-related litigation.

Limit your involvement with the group. Don't underestimate its ability to convert you. It is usually best not to give the member any money. This will be difficult for close friends and family members, just as it will be difficult for them not to humor the cult member. Basically, it seems to be most effective to take a relatively moderate position, focusing primarily on manipulation and deceptions in groups rather than on the irrationality of their belief systems.

(These suggestions for opening up communications with cult members are also useful in working with those who have come to believe some of the extraordinary pseudo-scientific and metaphysical claims made by various groups and individuals in our time.)

Educational Workshop

I have developed a workshop which aims to inoculate participants against involvement in destructive groups. One of the cornerstones of the workshop is a set of suggestions that I call "Ten Steps to Critical Thinking:"

1. Recognize demand situations that appear to require you to act in a certain way.

2. Remember that you can say "no."

3. Recognize false dilemmas. Always add "none of the above" to any multiple choice before deciding.

4. Sleep on it. Recognize pressure to decide quickly. Don't act under stress.

5. Look for the hidden agenda. What is really being said? What is not being said? To whom, by whom, and why is it being said?

6. Recognize logical fallacies.

7. Know what group or belief a person represents. Ask blunt questions and don't accept vague answers.

8. Recognize flattery.

9. Ask questions. Challenge authority claims.

10. Retain your sense of self-worth. Don't be afraid to be different.

Religion scholar Jacob Needleman has said that it's good to have an open mind, but not so open that your brains fall out. And Charlie Chan said that the mind is like a parachute--it functions only when it's open.

How to Talk to People Who are Trying to Save You

Rev. Dr. Ross Miller

They stop you on campus, knock on your door, waylay you on the street. They just want a few minutes of your time. . .to take a survey or talk about their faith. How do you respond to these sometimes aggressive folk?

1. *Be glad.* They're trying to do you good. After all, they want to keep you from eternal fire or some other undesirable end. You may not like their methods or message, but most of them mean well.

2. *Be careful.* Although many of these persons will respect your privacy, intelligence, and freedom, others are not necessarily eager to know what you think, believe, or feel. Their inquiries are calculated a), if they are Christian, to assess your salvation state (and any response that's halting or deviates from their pat formula will get you classified as "unsaved," even if you have Christian credentials like baptism, confirmation, church membership), and, presuming you flunk their test, b) to make you feel spiritually inadequate and in need of what they offer. These persons are more like salesmen than ethical evangelists, who witness to their faith in a respectful, loving manner.

3. *Don't expect dialogue.* Dialogue means a two-way sharing of ideas in an atmosphere of mutual respect. You'll soon learn that they have little interest in your views. They do not expect to find spiritual nourishment in your statements. (It is possible for persons of differing religious views to share ideas without attempting to trap or demean each other. Such an exchange can stimulate the growth of both participants.) Their goal is, as they say, "to win you to Christ," or to some guru or religious figure--a very competitive concept! And they feel very strongly that they are the authorities on "Christ," or whomever.

4. *Resist the temptation to debate!* In the first place, unless you're "well-versed" in Scripture and theology, you'll come off badly. And if you're ready to debate, be assured that your superior arguments will rarely convince them to change. (They might be surprised at someone as sure as they are, having mostly encountered the unsure and ignorant. But they'll most likely assume that the Devil's got you or that you're stuck in ignorance.) Furthermore, though debating may be fun, demolishing your opponent with argument may not be the outcome you want.

5. *Don't feel your experience of God is deficient if it doesn't fit their pattern.* For some persons, conversion (turning towards God) is sudden and emotionally overwhelming. Others experience a more gradual rebirthing and growth in faith. God's not stuck with a single strategy for changing humans. Christians and persons of other faiths--from the first through the twentieth century--testify to an amazing diversity of "divine styles."

6. *Don't worry if you can't answer questions!* Be wary of those who articulate a scheme of salvation or spiritual growth with the precision of an AAA map. All such simple "maps" must be taken for what they are: attempts to make the Divine Mystery comprehensible. Though we continually try to communicate our faith in understandable terms, we are always humbled by the limits of language in trying to grasp the Mystery we encounter. If their questions baffle and bother you, don't assume they're right and you're wrong. Share these questions with your pastor, or campus chaplain, rabbi, or priest (like checking *Consumer Reports* before you buy an encyclopedia).

7. *Ask questions of your own.* One of the problems with these "encounters" is their offensive/defensive nature--very offensive at times! Though debate or dialogue may not work, you can at least exchange information.

    Important: Don't try to trap them--that's their game. Your questions must be genuine. But don't let them use your questioning as just another means of persuading you to do what they want.

8. *Try to be kind and loving, without being foolish.* Remember, these persons trying to corner you (for the sincerest of reasons) are persons whom God loves. Despite their apparent strength, they may be needy persons whose involvement in an authoritarian group satisfies a strong dependency need. An awareness of their common humanity can save you from the trap they're setting, and, perhaps, help them see more clearly.

9. *Witness to your own faith.* You may not be able to support your testimony with scripture, but chances are you do have strong beliefs which have been nurtured through the years by teachers, pastors, priests, rabbis, parents, friends, and your own study and contemplation. You don't talk about these deep commitments very often, but they are

there. And you can witness to the values of your religious experience. Perhaps you appreciate its support in times of crisis, its involvement in making your community a better place, its serving real human needs, its music, etc.

10. *Be thankful.* This encounter will probably stimulate your spiritual search. It may encourage you to do more religious study. Perhaps you should thank your visitors for their help. But. . .

11. *Don't sign anything or agree to anything!* These folks trying to save you have been trained, just like salespeople, to talk you into some kind of "follow-up." They'd love to get you to one of their meetings. . ."just so you can give it a try." (If they haven't "won you" they'd like to get some help from their veteran persuaders--the folks who "won" them.) It's best to bid farewell with no strings. You can always find them if, after much reflection and discussion with friends or clergy, you decide to explore their group further.

Resources

Resources on Cults, Psychological Manipulation, and Satanism and Occult Ritual Abuse

Marcia R. Rudin, MA

This listing is the most current available at the date of publication. To obtain the most up-to-date list of resources and publications or to obtain prices and information about ordering procedures, contact the International Cult Education Program, P.O. Box 1232, Gracie Station, New York, NY 10028, (212) 439-1550.

Periodicals

* **Cult Awareness Network News.** Monthly newsletter containing cult news and Cult Awareness Network affiliate information. Published by the Cult Awareness Network (CAN).
* **The Cult Observer.** Press review published 10 times yearly of the legal, social, psychological, and medical aspects of cultism in society, published by the American Family Foundation (AFF). *Cult Observer* subscribers also receive, free of charge, *Young People and Cults: The Newsletter of the International Cult Education Program* (see below), AFF's Annual Report, and AFF News. *The Cult Observer* has reviewed over 2000 press accounts since 1979.
* **Cultic Studies Journal.** Bound scholarly journal, published semiannually, now in its eighth year of publication. The only scholarly journal dealing with cults and psychological manipulation. Averages approximately 100 pages/issue.
* **Young People and Cults: The Newsletter of the International Cult Education Program.** Semi-annual newsletter published by the International Cult Education Program (ICEP), providing news and advice to help clergy, educators, and others conduct preventive-education programs for youth. Free to *Cult Observer* subscribers and ICEP members.

Books

* **Combatting Cult Mind Control.** Steven Hassan, M.Ed. (1988). [Park Street Press.] 226 pages. General audiences, high schools, colleges and universities, churches, synagogues.
* **Cults & Consequences: The Definitive Handbook.** Rachel Andres & James R. Lane (Eds.) (1988). [Los Angeles, CA: Commission on Cults and Missionaries of the Jewish Federation Council of Greater Los

Angeles.] 250 pages. General audiences, high schools, colleges and universities, churches, synagogues.

* **Cults, Sects and the New Age**. Rev. James J. LeBar, with Revs. Kent Burtner, Walter Debold, and James McGuire. (1989) [Huntington, IN: Our Sunday Visitor Press.] 288 pages. General audiences, high schools, colleges, churches, synagogues. Of particular interest to Catholic readers.

* **Cults: What Parents Should Know**. Joan C. Ross, Ed.M., and Michael D. Langone, Ph.D. (1989). [Lyle Stuart, Inc.] 133 pages. General information about cults and communications-skills manual for communicating with cult members and those exiting from cults. General audiences, colleges and universities, churches, synagogues. Especially useful for families and friends of cult members and exiting cult members.

* **Satanism and Occult-Related Violence: What You Should Know**. Linda O. Blood and Michael D. Langone, Ph.D. (1990). [American Family Foundation.] Overview of satanism, with advice for parents and helping professionals. General audiences, parents, high schools, colleges, churches, synagogues, clergy, law enforcement officials, mental health professionals. Suitable reading for teenagers also.

* **Smashing the Idols: A Jewish Inquiry into the Cult Phenomenon**. Gary D. Eisenberg (Ed.). (1988). [Dunmore, PA: Jason Aronson, Inc.] 360 pages. Anthology of informative articles by experts. General audiences, high schools, colleges, churches, synagogues. Of particular interest to Jewish readers.

Reports

* **Bibliography on Satanism**. Linda O. Blood, 1989. Comprehensive bibliography and listing of occult-related crimes. 23 pages.

* **Business and the New Age Movement: Report of a Symposium**, 1987. (This report is included with the Business and New Age Movement Packet.) 4 pages.

* **Cracking the Riddle of the Cults: Frontiers of Freedom in an Information Age**. Flo Conway and Jim Siegelman (authors of *Snapping*), 1988. 12 pages.

* **Cult Involvement: Suggestions for Concerned Parents and Professionals**. Michael D. Langone, Ph.D., 1985. 20 pages.

* **Cultism: A Conference for Scholars and Policymakers**. Louis J. West, M.D. and Michael D. Langone, Ph.D., 1986. Report of a Wingspread conference conducted by AFF and UCLA's Neuropsychiatric Institute. 16 pages.

* **Cults Go To High School: A Theoretical and Empirical Analysis of the Initial Stage in the Recruitment Process.** Philip Zimbardo, Ph.D. and Cynthia Hartley, MA, 1985. 56 pages.
* **Cults: Questions and Answers.** Michael D. Langone, Ph.D., 1988. Succinct overview. 13 pages.
* **Cults: What Clergy Should Know.** Rev. Richard L. Dowhower, 1989. 4 pages.
* **Deprogramming: An Analysis of Parental Questionnaires.** Michael D. Langone, Ph.D., 1984. 54 pages.
* **Destructive Cult Conversion: Theory, Research, and Treatment.** John G. Clark, M.D. *et al.*, 1981. 84 pages.
* **Family Cult Questionnaire: Guidelines for Professionals.** Michael D. Langone, Ph.D., 1983. 31 pages.
* **How Cults Affect Families.** Henrietta and Curt Crampton, 1988. 4 pages.
* **New Religions and Public Policy: Research Implications for Social Scientists.** Michael D. Langone, Ph.D. and John G. Clark, M.D., 1984. 42 pages.
* **On Resisting Social Influence.** Susan Andersen, Ph.D. and Philip Zimbardo, Ph.D., 1984. 23 pages.

Information Packets

* **Bible-Based Groups.** Articles discussing cultic activities associated with aberrant Christian groups. Includes critiques by Evangelicals and the special report, *"Multiplying Ministries" Movement* by F.H. (Buddy) Martin, (copyright, Memorial Church of Christ, Houston, TX, 1987). 81 pages.
* **Business and the New Age Movement.** Press and trade journal reports describing how the New Age Movement has affected business. 75 pages.
* **Child Abuse in Cults.** A collection of articles detailing ways in which children have been abused and neglected in cultic groups. 35 pages.
* **Church/Synagogue Packet.** A collection of articles and reports about the effects of cults on established religious groups, including responses to this challenge. 45 pages.
* **Legal Packet.** Includes articles from the FBI Law Enforcement Bulletin, Vanderbilt Law Review, and other sources. 60 pages.
* **Mental Health Packet.** Includes articles from the Journal of the American Medical Association, Social Casework, and other professional sources. 75 pages.
* **Neo-Nazi Groups.** Press reports on cult-like groups such as the Aryan

Nations, Posse Comitatus, Skinheads. 65 pages.

* **New Age Movement.** Press reports on various aspects of the New Age Movement, including, for example, channeling. 70 pages.
* **Psychotherapy Cults.** Press reports and journal articles on how psychotherapy groups can become cults and on several specific groups, e.g., Center for Feeling Therapy, Synanon. 70 pages.
* **Satanism.** Newspaper and magazine articles, resource list, and other material documenting and analyzing the phenomenon. 60 pages.

Curricula and Course Plans

* **Cultivating "Cult-Evading": A Teacher's Guide.** Sandy Andron, Ed.D., 1983. Central Agency for Jewish Education, Miami. 44 pages. High schools, churches, synagogues.
* **Cults, Persuasion, and Human Vulnerability: A Syllabus for College and University Courses.** Joan Carol Ross, Ed.M., 1988. 10 pages. Supplemented by a course plan for cult-education in colleges and universities developed by Ronald N. Loomis, Director of Unions and Activities, Cornell University.
* **Seeking Information: Parts One and Two.** Brant W. Abrahamson. Published by The Teachers' Press. Curriculum designed to be taught in high schools over six to nine-week period by teachers at Brookfield High School, Brookfield, IL. Focuses on critical thinking and evaluation of information, with analysis of freedom and authority. Sections on cults, occultism, psychic phenomena, Eastern and Western religions, folk wisdom, humanities, sciences, and social sciences. Includes 116-page student text, 53-page student discussion guide and workbook, and 66-page teacher's manual with detailed instructions for library projects. Can be used also in colleges and universities, churches, and synagogues, and can be modified for shorter teaching time period.

Other Teaching Aids

* **Cults and Mind Control.** Four-page handout for high school and college students. Selections from key articles and a selected publication list.
* **Easily Fooled: New Insights and Techniques for Resisting Manipulation.** Robert C. Fellows, MTS. A magician explains the deceptions in everyday life and encourages critical thinking. Especially useful for young people.
* **How To Talk To People Who Are Trying To Save You.** Rev. Dr. Ross Miller. Four-page *Reader's Digest*-sized format.
* **Pseudoscience Fact Sheets: Resources to Promote Critical Thinking.**

Produced by the Austin Society to Oppose Pseudoscience and American Family Foundation, 1988. Brief papers on such topics as astrology, extrasensory perception, spiritualism, astral travel, and other subjects. 43 pages.
* **When You're Asked About Cults.** Robert C. Fellows, MTS. Four-page *Reader's Digest*-sized format.

Brochures

* **Could This Happen to You? A Guide to Making Safe Judgments About Groups on Campus.** Brochure prepared by the International Cult Education Program and the Cult Awareness Network for sale to colleges and universities for distribution to students. May be ordered with specific college or university and its resources printed on it. May order printed brochures or camera-ready artwork if the school wishes to print up the brochures itself. (Please direct inquiries to the Cult Awareness Network, address and telephone number in resource list below.)

Audio-Visual Resources

(Except for the ICEP videotape, "Cults: Saying *No* Under Pressure", these audio-visual resources cannot be ordered through the International Cult Education Program. Prices and ordering information are at the end of each entry.)

* **The Children's Story.** Excellent and gripping story by James Clavell of how impressionable minds can be taught what to think. Inspiration Films, 7200 S. Central Ave., Box 249, LaGrange, IL 60525, Tel. 800-323-4283 (film orders only) or 708-246-7990. 16mm rental, $39.00; video purchase, $29.95. 30 minutes.
* **Cults: Saying "No" Under Pressure.** Videotape developed by the International Cult Education Program and the InService Videotape Network of the National Association of Secondary School Principals, produced by Instructivision, Inc. Approximately twenty-five minutes. VHS only. Narrated by Charlton Heston. Focuses on deception, mind-manipulation, and pressure used to recruit and keep people in cults and how to resist these tactics. Brief discussion of participation of young people in occult rituals. For high school and college students, church and synagogue classes and youth groups, parents, educators, clergy, law enforcement officials, and others. Purchase only (no rental) $75.00, $59.00 for members of the International Cult Education

Program and contributors to the Cult Awareness Network and American Family Foundation. Add $2.50 per tape for postage and handling, $5.00 per tape for Canadian and overseas orders. International Cult Education Program, P.O. Box 1232, Gracie Station, New York, NY 10028. Tel. 212-439-1550.

* **In the Name of Satan: An In-Depth Look at Satanism with Host Bob Larson.** Videotape produced by Bob Larson Ministries. Forty minutes. VHS Only. No rental. Excellent introduction to satanic ritual abuse and teen satanism (focus on teens' serious and criminal involvement in satanism, not on teen "dabblers"). Includes interviews with therapists and other professionals, adult ritual abuse survivors, and former teen satanists. Non-religious orientation. May not be shown publicly without special permission from Bob Larson Ministries. Warning: not suitable for children. $19.95 plus $1.50 postage and handling. Bob Larson Ministries, P. O. Box 36-A, Denver, CO 80236.

* **Moonchild.** True story of a young man's recruitment by a cult, his involvement, and his exit. All actors are former cult members. Pyramid Films, Box 1048, Santa Monica, CA. 90406-1048, Tel. 800-421-2304 or 213-828-7577. 49 minutes. 2 reels (16mm film) $900.00; 1/2" Video (VHS) $225; 3/4" video, $275; film or video rental, $85 for three days.

* **Satanism: The Devil's Playground.** Videotape produced by Oblate Media & Communication. Forty-five minutes, broken into two segments. VHS. Introduction to satanism including warning signs, when to seek help, interviews with mental health professionals, law enforcement officials, Protestant and Catholic clergy, ritual abuse survivors, and former satanists, including teen participants. Slight religious orientation. Warning: Not suitable for children. $29.95. Includes brief Presenter's Guide. Oblate Media, 5901 West Main Street, Suite A, Belleville, IL 62223-4409, 1-800-233-4629, 618-277-4900, 618-235-8700.

* **Ticket To Heaven.** True story of a young man's experience in the Unification Church. Available for rent or purchase from most video stores.

* **Video Interviews with Ex-Unification Church Members.** By Michael Epstein.

    A) **What does Moon Want? 1988; Leaving Father, Going Home.** An intimate look at current Unification Church activities by two members who recently left the church: Ed Mignot, personally acquainted with Moon and high-level church operations, and Jorgen Pederson from Denmark.

    B) **Cults in the 80's: A European Perspective and Life in the Unification Church. Cults in the 80's: A European Perspective** is an interview with Anders Blichfeldt of the Dialogue Center of Aarhus, Denmark, in which he discusses current worldwide activities of several groups from sociological, psychological, religious, and legal perspectives. **Life in the Unification Church** is an interview with Eva Pehrsson, a Swedish woman who was recruited into the Unification church while visiting San Francisco in 1985.

Each pair of interviews is on a two-hour VHS tape. $29.95 each, including shipping and handling. Cult Awareness Network, 2421 West Pratt Blvd., Suite 1173, Chicago, IL 60645. Tel. 312-267-7777.

* **The Wave.** True story of a teacher's classroom experience when he drills power, discipline, and superiority into his surprisingly willing students. Available from Films, Inc./Education, 5547 N. Ravenswood Ave., Chicago, IL 60640-1199. Tel. 312-878-2600 (for Illinois) or 800-323-4222. 46 minutes. Purchase: $79 video, $750 film. Rental: $75.00 for one day. (Contact Chuck Fuller, ext. 388.)

Resource Organizations - Cults and Psychological Manipulation
(Listed Alphabetically According to Location)

Organizations, addresses, and telephone numbers are subject to change. To obtain the most up-to-date list of resource organizations, contact the International Cult Education Program. *Please note:* The International Cult Education Program in no way recommends or endorses any particular organization on the list; it merely presents them as available resources.

United States

* **Christian Research Institute**
Box 500
San Juan Capistrano, CA 92693
(714-855-9926)

* **Commission on Cults and Missionaries**
Jewish Federation Council of Greater Los Angeles
6505 Wilshire Blvd.
Los Angeles, CA 90048
(213-852-1234)

* **Cult Clinic**
Jewish Family Services of Los Angeles

6505 Wilshire Blvd., Suite 608
Los Angeles, CA 90048
(213-852-1234, x1650)

* **Spiritual Counterfeits Project**
PO Box 4308
Berkeley, CA 94704
(415-540-5767)

* **Religious Movement Resource Center**
629 S. Howes
Fort Collins, CO 80521
(303-482-8487)

* **American Family Foundation (AFF)**
PO Box 2265
Bonita Springs, FL 33959
(212-249-7693)

* **Committee on Cults and Missionaries**
Miami Jewish Federation
4200 Biscayne Blvd.
Miami, FL 33137
(305-576-4000)

* **Cult Awareness Network (CAN)** [national office]
2421 West Pratt Blvd., Suite 1173
Chicago, IL 60645
(312-267-7777)

* **FOCUS [Former Cultists Support Network]**
Contact Marty Butz,
Cult Awareness Network [national office]
see above

* **Humanistic Committee on Destructive Cults**
PO Box 626
Jamaica Plain, MA 02130
(617-522-7745)

* **Cult Clinic/Hot Line**
Jewish Board of Family and Childrens' Services

1651 Third Avenue
New York, NY 10028
(212-860-8533)

* **Interfaith Coalition of Concern About Cults (ICCC)**
  711 Third Avenue, 12th Floor
  New York, NY 10017
  (212-983-4977)

* **International Cult Education Program (ICEP)**
  PO Box 1232, Gracie Station
  New York, NY 10028
  (212-439-1550)

* **Task Force on Missionaries and Cults**
  Jewish Community Relations Council (JCRC) of New York
  711 Third Avenue, 12th Floor
  New York, NY 10017
  (212-983-4800)

* **Wellspring Retreat and Resource Center**
  PO Box 67
  Albany, OH 45710
  (614-698-6277)

* **RETIRN**
  9887 Verree Rd.
  Philadelphia, PA 19115
  (215-698-8900)

* **Bothered About Dungeons and Dragons**
  P.O. Box 5513
  Richmond, VA 23220-0513
  (804-264-0403)

Canada and Overseas

* **Association Exposing Pseudo-Religious Cults**
  Box 900 G
  Melbourne 3001
  AUSTRALIA

*   **Freedom of Choice**
    University of Melbourne
    Box 4020
    Parkville 3052
    AUSTRALIA

*   **Concerned Christian Growth Ministries**
    Box 6
    North Perth 6006
    WESTERN AUSTRALIA
    (61634446183)

*   **The Jewish Centre**
    Box 34 (Melbourne)
    Balaclava, Victoria 3183
    AUSTRALIA
    (6135275069)

*   **Gesamtosterreichische Elterninitiative**
    Obere Augartenstrasse
    A-1020 Wien
    AUSTRIA

*   **ADFI**
    Hertogenweg 8
    1980 Tervuen
    BELGIUM
    (3227675421)

*   **Instituto Cristao de Pesquisas**
    (Christian Research Institute - Brazil)
    Caixa Postal 5011 -- Agencia Central
    01051 Sao Paulo, SP
    BRASIL
    (55112564801)

*   **Alberta Cult Education**
    10136-100 Street, Suite 502
    Edmonton, Alberta T5P 4C1
    CANADA
    (403-476-9601)

* **Council on Mind Abuse**
  40 St. Clair Ave., East
  Toronto, Ontario M4T 1M9
  CANADA
  (416-944-0080)

* **Info-Cult** [formerly "Cult Project"]
  5655 Park Avenue, 305
  Montreal, Quebec H2V 4H2
  CANADA
  (514-274-2333)

* **SCAMC**
  Meadow Lake Chapter
  Box 358
  Meadow Lake, Saskatchwan SCM IVO
  CANADA

* **Christian Research Institute - Canada**
  P.O. Box 3216 Station "B"
  Calgary, Alberta T2M 4L7
  CANADA
  (403-277-7702)

* **The Dialog Center**
  Katrinebjergve 46
  Aarhus, N, DK-8200
  DENMARK
  (456105411)

* **Cult Information Centre**
  BCM Cults
  London WC1N 3XX
  ENGLAND
  (0816513322)

* **Cultists Anonymous**
  BM Box 1407
  London WC1N 3XX
  ENGLAND
  (0482443104)

* **Deo Gloria Outreach**
  212-220 Addington Rd.
  South Croydon, Surrey CR2 8LD
  ENGLAND
  (0816516430)

* **FAIR**
  BCM Box 3535 - P.O. Box 12
  London, WC1N 3XX
  ENGLAND
  (4415393940)

* **ADFI (Association Pour la Defense de L'Individu et de la Famille)**
  10 Rue du Pere Julien Dhuit
  75020 Paris
  FRANCE
  (47979608)

* **Centre de Documentation d'Education et d'Action Contre Les Manipulations Mentales**
  19 rue Turgot
  75009 Paris
  FRANCE
  (42820493)

* **EHSARE**
  PO Box 874
  D-8000 Munchen 1
  GERMANY

* **Pan-Hellenic Parents' Union for the Protection of the Family and the Individual**
  14 Ioannou Gennadiou St.
  Athens 11521
  GREECE

* **Concerned Parents**
  Box 1806
  Haifa 31018
  ISRAEL
  (9724718522)

* **ARIS (Associazione per la Ricerca e L'informazione sulle Sette)**
  Via A. Doria, 913
  20058 Villasanta
  ITALY
  (039306070)

* **GRIS (Gruppo di Ricerca e di Informazione sulle Sette)**
  Via del Monte 5
  40126 Bologna
  ITALY
  (051260011)

* **SOS**
  255G Graafsweg 5213
  AJ S'Hertogenbosch
  NETHERLANDS
  (31836028773)

* **Asociacion Pro Juventud**
  A.I.S. (Asesoramiento e Informacion sobre Sectas)
  Aribau, 226
  08006 Barcelona
  SPAIN
  (3432014886)

* **CROAS (Centro de Rehabilitacion, Orientacion y Ayuda a Sectarios)**
  [support group for cultists, associated with Asociacion Pro Juventud]
  see above

* **SADK (Schweizerische Arbeitsgemeinschaft gegen Destruktive Kulte)**
  Postfach 18
  8156 Oberhasli
  SWITZERLAND
  (071756107)

* **Cult Awareness Project**
  Church of Sweden
  Box 438
  75106 Uppsala
  SWEDEN

*   **Foreningen Radda Individen**
Langholmsgatan 17
11733 Stockholm
SWEDEN
(086684713)

Resource Organizations - Satanism and
Occult Ritual Abuse
(Listed Alphabetically According to Location)

Most of the above-listed resource organizations can also provide information and expertise about satanism and occult ritual abuse. Below are organizations *specializing* in information and assistance concerning these topics. To obtain a complete and updated list such individuals and organizations, contact the International Cult Education Program. *Please note:* The International Cult Education Program in no way recommends or endorses any particular organization on the list; it merely presents them as available resources.

*   **Monarch Resources**
PO Box 1293
Torrence, CA 90505-0293
213-373-1958
[Information, publications, counseling of ritual-abuse survivors]

*   **People Against Satanic Teaching (PAST)**
PO Box 321
Lower Sackville, Nova Scotia B42 2T2
CANADA
(902) 864-2297
[Counseling]

*   **Fair Oaks Hospital**
19 Prospect Street
Summit, NJ 07902-0100
(201) 277-9121
[Assessment, counseling of adolescents]

*   **Four Winds Hospital**
Cross River Road
Katonah, NY 10536

(914) 763-8151
[Twenty-bed treatment unit]

* **Genesis Associates**
663 Exton Commons
Exton, PA 19341
(212-363-2966)
[Counseling]

* **Beyond, Inc.**
7124 Forest Hill Ave., Suite G
Richmond, VA 23225
(804) 272-9472
[Counseling - dissociative disorders and ritual abuse]

Ritual Abuse Support Groups

* **The RAP Line (Ritual Abuse Phone Line)**
PO Box 1476
Lomita, CA 90717
(213) 370-7459
[Hours: 8 am - 10 pm or call-back within 24 hours]

* **Survivorship**
3181 Mission Street, #139
San Francisco, CA 94110
[A forum on survival of ritual abuse, torture, and mind control.
Provides resource list.]

* **Christian Survivors of Ritual Abuse (CSRA)**
PO Box 48451
Wichita, KS 67201
[Correspondence group for therapists, clergy and survivors seeking
healing from ritual abuse from a Christian perspective]

* **Vineyard**
Box 3475
Tega Cay, SC 29715

Ritual Abuse Research Groups

*   **Task Force on Ritual Abuse**
    Los Angeles County Commission for Women
    383 Hall of Administration
    500 W. Temple St.
    Los Angeles, CA 90012
    (213) 974-1455

*   **CARAC (Committee Against Ritual Abuse of Children)**
    P. O. Box 74
    Saskatoon, Saskatchewan S7K 3K1
    CANADA
    (306) 966-8500